COLORS

from

NATURE

Growing, Collecting and Using Natural Dyes

BY BOBBI A. MCRAE

A STOREY PUBLISHING BOOK

Storey Communications, Inc.
Schoolhouse Road
Pownal, Vermont 05261

Edited by Gwen W. Steege
Cover and text design by Cindy McFarland
Production assistance by Andrea Gray and Susan Bernier
Cover photographs by Nicholas Whitman
Text photographs by Nicholas Whitman and Cindy McFarland
Line drawings by Brigita Fuhrmann, except for the following:
   Polly Alexander, p. 68 (right); Judy Eliason, p. 64; Charles
   Joslin, pp. 72, 73 (top left), 75, 77, 79, 80 (bottom left), 86;
   Alison Kolesar, pp. 65 (bottom left), 144; Mallory Lake, pp. 66
   (left), 73 (bottom left), 80 (top left), 81 (left)
Indexed by Gail Damerow

The information in this book is true and complete to the best of our knowledge. All recommendations are made without guarantee on the part of the author or Storey Communications, Inc. The author and publisher disclaim any liability in connection with the use of this information. For additional information please contact Storey Communications, Inc., Schoolhouse Road, Pownal, Vermont 05261.

Printed in the United States by The Book Press

First Printing, April 1993

Library of Congress Cataloging-in-Publication Data
McRae, Bobbi A.
    Colors from nature : growing, collecting, and using natural dyes / Bobbi A. McRae.
            p.   cm.
        Includes bibliographical references and index.
        ISBN 0-88266-806-4 (hc) — ISBN 0-88266-799-8 (pbk.)
        1. Dyes and dyeing{m}Textile fibers.   2. Dyes and dyeing, Domestic.   3. Dye plants.   I. Title.
    TT854.3.M38   1993
    667'.26—dc20   92-53808
                            CIP

contents

Preface v
Acknowledgments vii

Part I **Introduction to Natural Dyeing 1**

1 ◆ *What Are Natural Dyes 3*
2 ◆ *Preparation for Dyeing 28*
3 ◆ *Mordants and Mordanting 37*
4 ◆ *Dyeing Natural Fibers 50*

Part II **The Dyes and Where to Get Them 61**

5 ◆ *Dyes to Gather 63*
6 ◆ *Dyes from Your Garden 70*
7 ◆ *Dyes from the Grocery Store 83*
8 ◆ *Dyes to Order 86*

Part III **Projects Using Natural Dyes on Natural Fibers 93**

Around-the-World Needlepoint Pillow 95
Baby's First Garden Crocheted Blanket and Pillow 99
Counted Cross-Stitch Dye Plant Notecards 102
Woven Wool Tapestry 106
Sewn-Wool Fabric Rug 109
Quilted Cotton Wall Hanging 112
Batik on Silk 115
Handmade Notepapers from Recycled Paper 118
Color Section 121
Felt Purse with Silk Lining 129
Confetti Splint Basket 133
Cornhusk Wreath 137
Cornhusk Angel 140
Naturally Dyed Easter Eggs 143

APPENDIXES 145

Note on Copying and Enlarging Patterns 147
Mail-Order Suppliers 148
Suggested Reading 150
Credits 151
Glossary 152

INDEX 153

Preface

Book ideas sometimes come to authors in round-about ways. After compiling the bibliography for my book *Nature's Dyepot: A Resource Guide for Spinners, Weavers and Dyers,* I realized that although much has been written about natural dyeing, much of it is out of print and thus difficult to obtain. I had been using herbs from my own garden to color handmade paper, and I became intrigued by the possibilities of using them to dye yarns. Then, while compiling the bibliography, I came across a color photo in *Dyes from Nature,* edited by Rita Buchanan, of a breathtakingly beautiful cotton quilt dyed by Jim Lilies. I had never seen such beautiful colors on cotton fabrics and was instantly smitten. I decided then and there to write a different type of dye book—one for beginners and experienced dyers that would take a fresh approach to the subject by emphasizing experimentation and avoiding specific recipes. I was particularly excited about trying these dyes on basketry materials, needlepoint yarns, and cotton embroidery threads, since little had been written about these fibers. I also wanted to include original projects using these materials.

Because of the many books and articles about natural dyes that have been written over the past twenty or thirty years, the more I read, the more

I realized that it would be hard to find new things to say about this subject. At times, all of the books started to sound the same, and indeed, many of them were.

Since I was approaching my book as a beginning natural dyer (although I had used synthetic dyes), my method was to read everything that I could find on the subject, both books and magazine articles. From there, I made a basic listing of plants that were readily available and started experimenting with them. I then started growing some of the plants in my own garden and gathered or ordered what I could not grow. Friends from around the country sent me dried dyestuffs to try, and I was therefore able to include a greater number of plants.

I decided that although wool and, to some extent, silk had been covered thoroughly, little had been written about dyeing other materials, such as cornhusks or basketry materials, with natural dyes. My work in this area is wholly original, with only a few notes from dyers across the country to guide me. I was successful in actually dyeing these materials with plants, as you can see by the results in the color photos included in this book.

For those techniques and ideas I used that are not original, I would like to recognize a few of the contemporary authors who have put in countless hours of experimentation, and who have worked hard to eradicate the many myths and misconceptions about the process of natural dyeing that appear and reappear in some of the older books. These people were especially instrumental in getting me interested in the subject in the first place, and I have relied on their written works as sources of authentic, correct information. Their methods have, for the most part, been published in the books that you will find listed in the appendix. These are, in alphabetical order, Anne Bliss, Rita Buchanan, Karen Casselman, Jim N. Liles, Dorothy Miller, and Ruth Pierce.

Anne Bliss has written several extremely useful books about using common plants (both wild and cultivated) as dyes. Her many delightful articles on the subject have appeared in past issues of *Handwoven* magazine. I found her plant identification manuals extremely useful when I gathered plants from the wild.

Rita Buchanan was the first contemporary author to relate the importance of plants to the lives of textile artists. Although Ms. Buchanan is a botanist, horticulturist, and all-round fiber arts expert, she has the gift of explaining complicated techniques and methods so that they are understandable to the layperson. She also knows how to make a plant "come alive" for the reader.

Karen Casselman wrote the exhaustive study of dye plants in the Northeast (including Canada), and her published information on lichens remains one of the most comprehensive in existence.

Jim N. Liles was the first to thoroughly investigate the use of traditional dyes (especially the mineral dyes) on cottons and linens. His work with authentic traditional costumes is phenomenal; he practices what he preaches.

Dorothy Miller has written the classic book on growing, gathering, and using Japanese indigo *(Polygonum tinctorium)*, an alternative to the more well-known *Indigofera tinctoria*.

Ruth Pierce has grown and used madder for many, many years and is not afraid to share her knowledge (and her seeds) with others.

I owe a debt of gratitude to all of these contemporary dyers and others who have contributed to the craft and keep it alive. I would like to thank them personally for their dedication to the subject.

Acknowledgments

◆ For my husband, Rudy Chukran — who put up with 6 months of dripping fabrics and fibers in the house and never once said "I told you so"

◆ For my mother, Barbara A. Neal, for giving up her polyester yarns long enough to crochet the "Baby's First Garden" blanket for me

◆ For Gwen Steege, my editor at Storey Communications, for her enthusiasm, helpful suggestions, and patience

◆ For Colleen Belk, Austin Herb Society president and friend

◆ For Suzanne Middlebrooks, owner of Hill Country Weavers in Austin, Texas, for valuable advice along the way

◆ For Susanna Reppert of The Rosemary House and Jim Bennett of Deer Track Crafts for sharing their experiences with dyeing basketry materials

I would also like to thank the many suppliers who donated materials for the projects in this book:

Rachel Brown of Rio Grande Weaver's Supply; Linda Urquhart of Rumpelstiltskin; Don McGill of Creek Water Wool Works; Ron and Teresa Parker of Sammen Sheep Farms; Henry and Samira Galler of Henry's Attic Yarns; Susan Bates, Inc.; Mr. James Bailey, Produce Manager at IGA Food Fare, Keller, Texas, for saving (and sorting by color) onion skins for me; Frontier Cooperative Herbs; Yarn Tree Designs, Inc.; Willmaur Crafts Corporation; and Testfabrics.

I would especially like to thank the herb suppliers that took time out of their busy schedules to send me plants for my dye garden — Taylor's Herb Gardens, Inc.; Louise Hyde of Well Sweep Herb Farm; and Gilbert A. Bliss of Wyrttun Ward.

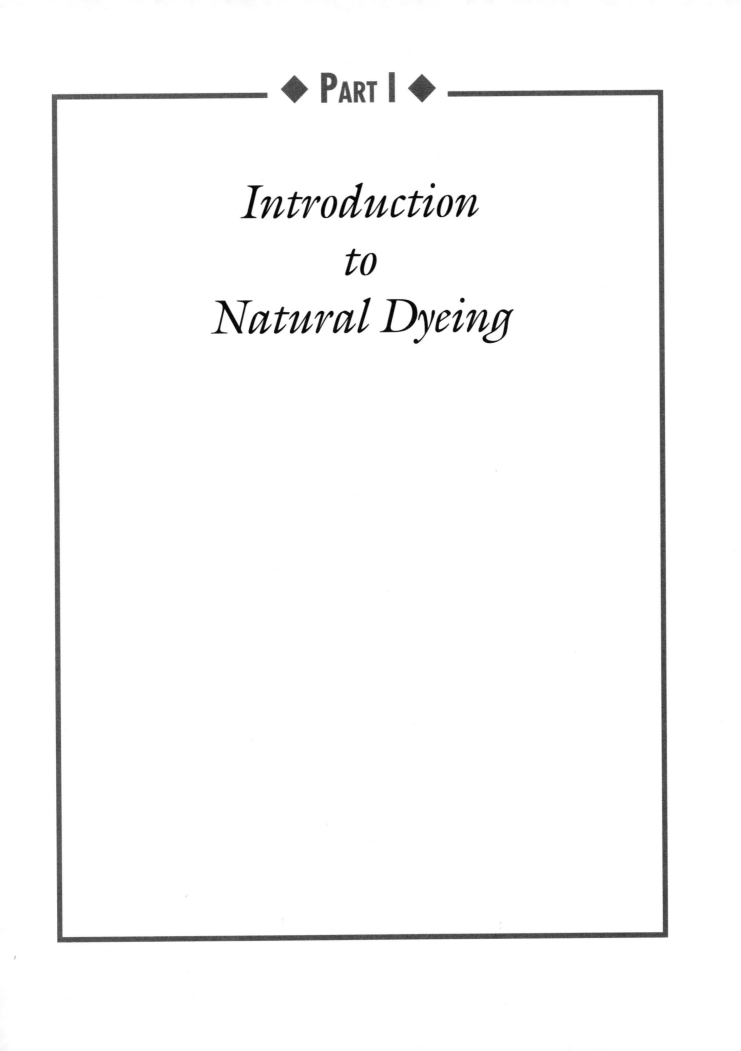

◆ PART I ◆

Introduction to Natural Dyeing

chapter 1

What Are Natural Dyes?

*t*he story of natural dyeing is as old as history itself. No one really knows how or when inhabitants of ancient civilizations first discovered that natural materials produce colors. Some anthropologists think that the discovery of natural dyes had its beginning in accidental stains left by the juices of berries, roots, or nuts. Eventually, these stains were used deliberately to dye skin and clothing .

Textile remnants dating from around 3,500 B.C. found in the tombs of Thebes show traces of blue from indigo. It is thought that early Egyptians even experimented with dyeing live sheep. Shirley Held relates in her book *Weaving* that Virgil thought that a sheep fed on madder would produce red wool!

In 1548, Gioanventura Rosetti of Venice wrote and published the first complete book of dye recipes, which he had gathered over the course of sixteen years from many Italian cities. His book, *The Plictho-Instructions in the art of the dyers which teaches the dyeing of woolen cloths, linens, cottons, and silk by the Great Art as well as by the Common,* included many previously guarded dye methods.

Throughout history, dyes, stains, and colors made from plants have been used for a variety of purposes. Natural dyes were used not only for the dyeing of yarns and fabrics but also as watercolors and in everyday cosmetics. The women of ancient Greece dyed their hair with a plant called thapsus *(Thapsia asclepium).* Centuries later, in 1551, William Turner's *New Herbal* speaks of marigolds: "Summe use to make theyr here [hair] yellow with the flowre of this herb not beyng content with the naturall colour which God hath given them."

The synthetic age of dyeing began in the mid-1800s when Sir Henry Perkin accidentally discovered the first aniline dye while trying to synthesize quinine. He called the light lavender color *mauvine,* and his discovery eventually led to the development of a whole new form of dyes, all synthetically manufactured.

Why Use Natural Dyes?

You may wonder, why bother to use natural dyes? I enjoy using natural dyes for several reasons, but they all boil down to my love for color. The heathery colors glow and blend with one another the same way the color of grass blends with that of trees. Seemingly alive, they reflect the light in interesting ways. The subtle colors seem always to harmonize with each other. One-of-a-kind colors become mellower, softer, and more beautiful with the passage of time. Before I began using natural dyes, I would never have used purple and gold shades in the same project. I now mix them freely, and find they belong together!

Of course, you can go to the nearest weaving or knitting shop and find many beautiful yarns in thousands of colors that have already been "pre-colored" for your convenience. But there is something primitively satisfying about taking a sackful of weeds destined for the compost pile and re-routing them into your dyepot to make something useful out of them.

Serendipity and the Dyepot

Experimentation and personal discovery are the main points that I would like to stress in this book. Most dye books are filled with precise recipes. These books certainly have their place, and many dyers have learned from them. Therefore, if you only glance through this book, you may be puzzled by the lack of strict, ounce-by-ounce recipes. The methods I outline in this book are a bit more haphazard and informal than most; I have included very few strict recipes. Instead, I have tried to provide basic instructions and simple rules that can be applied to all dyestuffs — flowers, roots, barks, leaves, or extracts — on all natural fibers, not just wool. (One of the few exceptions to this approach is the advice about indigo.)

For instance, the Mordanting Chart (pages 40–41) indicates exactly what each mordant does. You can thus deduce which one is appropriate for the effect you want, without needing a list of which mordants to use with which plants. This chart is the key to the book. The basic instructions for mordanting that I give are, for the most part, applicable to all types of natural fibers — wools, as well as cotton, linen, silk, and even basketry fibers. After a few experiments, you'll get a feel for what works and what doesn't work. You can build on this basic foundation with your own experimentation.

To open up your eyes to new possibilities, I've included some plants that you might not find listed in other dye books — for example, herbs such as mint and sage. Both make lovely greenish yellow colors on wool. Be creative and try something different!

I haven't listed every possible color that can be obtained from the featured plants. Instead, I conducted random tests of plants and dyestuffs on various natural fibers (including unusual ones, like cornhusks, raffia, cotton, and sisal) and listed a few of the resulting colors to give you an idea of the color range produced by the specified plants. It's up to you to discover the rest. Because of many possible variables, which I also discuss, your colors will probably be different from mine, anyway. In my experience, it's hard to duplicate colors, even when using strict recipes. For beginning dyers, I don't feel that this is a problem — it's more important to grasp the basics of the craft.

I also think that when you are not following strict, by-the-book recipes you have more room for adventure, inspiration — and fun! Some of your experiments will be disappointing, but many will produce beautiful and useful colors. I choose to accept the uncertainty, along with the surprises and disappointments, of using natural colors — and I've had more delightful surprises than disappointments in my experiments for this book.

Sources of Natural Dyes

Natural dyes derive from one of three sources: plants, animals, and minerals. Plant dyes include indigo, weld, and turmeric. Animal dyes include cochineal dyes from insects or the historically used Tyrian purple from mollusks. In this book, I emphasize plant dyes and only one animal dye — cochineal. Mineral dyes are substances from the earth, such as iron, copper, manganese, lead, chrome, and zinc. Chemical reactions between these minerals and various mordants have been used traditionally to color fibers. The oldest of these dyes is probably iron oxide, or rust. Jim N. Liles's book *The Art and Craft of Natural Dyeing: Traditional Recipes for Modern Use* contains a thorough, fascinating explanation of mineral dyes.

Ancient writers recorded that there were once nearly a thousand different sources of natural dyes, but because of the secrecy surrounding their recipes, many of them have been lost forever.

By the 1800s, home dyers had twenty different dyestuffs at their disposal, but used only nine predominantly. These nine dyes — madder, cochineal, indigo, woad, logwood, fustic, weld, safflower, and saffron — are still being used by dyers today, almost 200 years later. What is striking to me about this list is that very few new dyes have been added. Have we discovered all of the possible dyeplants in the world? I think not. You may discover something special that no one has ever used before — all it takes is time, a curious nature, and a little serendipity.

THE BASIC DYEPLANT CHART

This chart was complied from notes on my own experiments and the experiments of recognized authorities. The plants marked with an asterisk (*) are those that I have worked with; the remainder of the chart is drawn from information in various published sources. Those that I found especially helpful were *Natural Dyes and Home Dyeing*, by Rita J. Adrosko; *A Handbook of Dyes from Natural Materials*, by Anne Bliss; *Dyes from Nature*, edited by Rita Buchanan; *Craft of the Dyer*, by Karen Leigh Casselman; *The Art and Craft of Natural Dyeing*, by Jim N. Liles; and *A Practical Guide to Edible and Useful Plants*, by Delena Tull. (For complete bibliographic information see Suggested Reading, page 150.) This chart lists only a few of the many dye sources and colors that you can obtain from them. Use it as a guide to the color ranges possible with each plant; your colors will probably be slightly different. By all means, try plants that do not appear on this list. Record notes about your experiments in the space provided. If you wish to share your results, please do so for possible inclusion in future editions of this book.

DYE MATERIAL	COLOR	MORDANT	FIBER	PART USED
Absinthe (common wormwood), *Artemisia absinthium*				
	yellowish green	alum	wool	leaves
	gold	chrome	wool	leaves

THE BASIC DYEPLANT CHART (CONT'D)

DYE MATERIAL	COLOR	MORDANT	FIBER	PART USED
Absinthe (cont'd)				
	light green	copper	wool	leaves
	khaki	iron	wool	leaves
NOTES				

*Agrimony (church steeples, sticklewort, cockleburr), *Agrimonia eupatoria*

	COLOR	MORDANT	FIBER	PART USED
	gold	chrome	wool	leaves/stems (fresh)
	brassy yellow	alum	wool/cotton	leaves/stems (fresh)
	orange	tin	wool	leaves/stems (fresh)
	dark green	iron	wool	leaves/stems (fresh)
	yellow	alum	wool/silk	whole plant
NOTES				

Alder, *Alnus* species

	COLOR	MORDANT	FIBER	PART USED
	yellow	alum	wool	leaves
	yellowish green	alum+copper	wool	leaves
	tan	iron	wool	leaves
	rosy brown	chrome	wool	bark/twigs
	dark brown	iron	wool	bark/twigs
NOTES				

Alkanet, *Anchusa tinctoria*

	COLOR	MORDANT	FIBER	PART USED
	reddish purple	alum	wool	roots
NOTES				

Amaranth (Hopi red dye, pigweed), *Amaranthus* species

	COLOR	MORDANT	FIBER	PART USED
	light yellow	alum	wool	whole plant
NOTES				

THE BASIC DYEPLANT CHART (CONT'D)

DYE MATERIAL	COLOR	MORDANT	FIBER	PART USED
*Annatto (arnatto, urucu, achiote, roucou), *Bixa orellana*				
	bright yellow	none	wool	seeds
	reddish orange	alum	silk fabric	seeds
	bright orange	none	silk yarn	seeds
	light peach	alum/tannin	cotton embroidery floss	seeds
NOTES				
*Apple, *Malus* species				
	warm tan	chrome	wool	leaves
	brown	chrome	wool	leaves
	rusty brown	chrome	wool	leaves
	beige	none	wool	bark
	warm brown	none	wool	bark
	tannish yellow	none	wool	bark
NOTES				
Ash, *Fraxinus americana*				
	light yellow	alum	wool	leaves
	bright yellow	tin	wool	leaves
	rosy tan	alum+chrome	wool	bark
	brown	chrome	wool	bark
NOTES				
*Asparagus, *Asparagus officinalis*				
	yellow	tin	wool	plant (in fall)
NOTES				

THE BASIC DYEPLANT CHART (CONT'D)

DYE MATERIAL	COLOR	MORDANT	FIBER	PART USED
Aspen, *Populus* species				
	yellow	alum	wool	leaves
	yellow-orange	tin	wool	leaves
	gold	chrome	wool	leaves
NOTES	_____			
	_____			
Aster, *Aster* species				
	yellow	alum	wool	fresh blooms
	yellowish green	copper+iron	wool	fresh blooms
	tan	chrome	wool	fresh blooms
NOTES	_____			
	_____			
*****Barberry,** *Berberis* species				
	bright yellow	none	wool	twigs, leaves
	yellow	none	wool, silk	bark
	deep yellow	tin	wool	root
NOTES	_____			
	_____			
Bayberry, *Myrica pensylvanica*				
	yellow	alum	wool	leaves
	gold	chrome	wool	leaves
	bright yellow	tin	wool	leaves
NOTES	_____			
	_____			
*****Bedstraw (Lady's) (cheese rennet, Our Lady's bedstraw),** *Galium verum*				
	dull red	alum	wool	roots
	red	chrome	wool	roots
	light orange-red	alum+chrome	wool	roots
	purple-red	chrome+iron	wool	roots

THE BASIC DYEPLANT CHART (CONT'D)

DYE MATERIAL	COLOR	MORDANT	FIBER	PART USED
*Bedstraw (Lady's) (cont'd)				
	bluish gray	baking soda	wool	roots
	yellow	alum	wool	stems and tops
	plum	iron	wool	roots
NOTES				
Beech, *Fagus grandifolia*				
	yellow	alum	wool	leaves
	rust	tin	wool	leaves
	brown	chrome+tin	wool	bark
	gold	chrome	wool	leaves
NOTES				
Betony, *Stachys officinalis*				
	chartreuse	alum	wool	all parts
NOTES				
*Bindweed (creeping jenny, field bindweed), *Convolvulus arvensis*				
	yellow	alum	wool	whole plant
	dull green	copper	wool	whole plant
	khaki green	alum	wool	whole plant
	beige	none	wool	whole plant
NOTES				
Birch, *Betula* species				
	yellow	alum	wool	leaves
NOTES				

DYE MATERIAL	COLOR	MORDANT	FIBER	PART USED
*Black walnuts, *Juglans nigra*				
	green	chrome	wool	bark
	brown	none	wool, cotton	leaves
	light brown	none	wool, cotton	hulls, dried
	dark brown	chrome	wool	hulls, dried
	light brown	copper	wool	bark
	brownish black	chrome	wool	hulls, dried
NOTES				
*Brazilwood, *Caesalpinia echinata* or *Haematoxylum brasiletto*				
	red-lavender	none	wool	sawdust
	bright red	alum	wool	sawdust
	purple	chrome	wool	sawdust
	bright pink	tin	wool	sawdust
	blue-violet	alum+baking soda	wool	sawdust
	purple	alum+tannin	cotton embroidery floss	sawdust
NOTES				
Broom (dyer's), (dyer's greenwood, woadwaxen, greenweed, summer broom), *Genista tinctoria*				
	yellow	alum	wool	tops
	bright yellow	chrome	wool	flowers/leaves
NOTES				
Burdock, *Arctium minus*				
	yellow	alum	wool	leaves
	tan	alum+vinegar	wool	leaves
	bright yellow	tin	wool	leaves
NOTES				

THE BASIC DYEPLANT CHART (CONT'D)

DYE MATERIAL	COLOR	MORDANT	FIBER	PART USED
*Cabbage (purple), *Brassica* species				
	pinkish beige	alum	wool	whole head
	gray-lavender	none	silk	whole head
	mauve	none	silk	whole head
	light lavender	alum	DMC needle-point wools	whole head
	bright purple	alum+tannin	cornhusks	whole head
NOTES	_____			
	_____			
Carrot, *Daucus carota sativa*				
	greenish yellow	alum	wool	tops
	bright yellow	tin	wool	tops
NOTES	_____			
	_____			
*Catnip, *Nepeta cataria*				
	light yellow	alum	wool	leaves (in fall)
	grayish yellow	tin	wool	leaves (in fall)
NOTES	_____			
	_____			
Cedar, *Juniperus virginiana*				
	purple	alum	wool	roots
NOTES	_____			
	_____			
*Chamomile, *Anthemis nobilis*				
	golden-yellow	chrome	wool	flowers
	bright yellow	alum	wool	flowers
	olive green	iron	wool	flowers

DYE MATERIAL	COLOR	MORDANT	FIBER	PART USED
Chamomile (cont'd)				
	yellow-green	copper	wool	flowers
	maize	none	paper pulp	flowers
NOTES				
Chamomile (dyer's), *Anthemis tinctoria*				
	creamy yellow	alum	wool	flowers
	bright yellow	alum	wool	flowers
	bright orange	chrome	wool	flowers
	gold	chrome	wool	flowers
	clear yellow	tin	wool	flowers
	greenish yellow	alum+iron	wool	flowers
	khaki	alum+chrome	wool	flowers
NOTES				
Chrysanthemum, *Chrysanthemum* species				
	gold-yellow	alum	wool	leaves
	green	alum	wool (natural gray)	leaves
	gray-turquoise	alum	wool/cotton	flowers (maroon)
	yellow-green	alum	wool	young shoots
	green	chrome	wool	young shoots
	bronze	tin	wool	flowers (red)
NOTES				
*Cochineal, *Dactylopius coccus* (insect)				
	purple-red	alum	wool or silk	whole bugs
	light purple-red	alum	linen or cotton	whole bugs
	bright red	tin	wool or silk	whole bugs
	light red	tin	linen or cotton	whole bugs
	light magenta	alum	wool fabric	whole bugs

THE BASIC DYEPLANT CHART (CONT'D)

DYE MATERIAL	COLOR	MORDANT	FIBER	PART USED
*Cochineal (cont'd)				
	pink	alum+tannin	cornhusks	whole bugs
	light pink	none	paper pulp	whole bugs
	dark pink	alum+tannin	basketry splint	whole bugs
NOTES				
*Coffee, *Coffea arabica*				
	tan	alum+vinegar	wool	grounds
	tan	alum	cotton fabric	grounds
	medium brown	chrome	wool	grounds
	grayish tan	iron	wool	grounds
	greenish brown	alum+iron	wool	grounds
	dark tan	none	raffia	grounds
NOTES				
Coltsfoot, *Tussilago farfara*				
	greenish-yellow	alum	wool	leaves
	green	alum+copper	wool	leaves
	taupe	iron	wool	leaves
NOTES				
*Comfrey, *Symphytum officinale*				
	brown	iron	wool	leaves
NOTES				
Coneflower (Black-eyed Susan — *Rudbeckia hirta***),** *Rudbeckia* species				
	pale yellow	alum	wool	whole plant (not roots)
	green	alum	wool	flower heads

THE BASIC DYEPLANT CHART (CONT'D)

DYE MATERIAL	COLOR	MORDANT	FIBER	PART USED
Coneflower (cont'd)				
	greenish gold	chrome	wool	flower heads
	golden yellow	chrome	wool	flower petals only
	olive green	iron	wool	heads/leaves
NOTES				

DYE MATERIAL	COLOR	MORDANT	FIBER	PART USED
Coreopsis, calliopsis (dyer's coreopsis, tickseed), *Coreopsis tinctoria				
	brick red	chrome	wool	flowers
	dark red	chrome	wool	flowers
	tomato orange	alum	wool	flowers
	bright yellow	tin	wool	flowers
	golden brown	alum	wool	seed heads
	gold	alum+tannin	cotton	flowers
			embroidery floss	
NOTES				

DYE MATERIAL	COLOR	MORDANT	FIBER	PART USED
Cosmos, *Cosmos sulphureus				
	orange	chrome	wool	flowers
	yellow	tin	wool	flowers
NOTES				

DYE MATERIAL	COLOR	MORDANT	FIBER	PART USED
Cranberry, *Vaccinium macrocarpon				
	pink	alum	wool	berries
	reddish gold	tin	wool	berries
NOTES				

DYE MATERIAL	COLOR	MORDANT	FIBER	PART USED
Currant, *Ribes* species				
	purple	alum	wool	fruit (black)
	reddish brown	alum	wool	fruit (red)
NOTES				

THE BASIC DYEPLANT CHART (CONT'D)

DYE MATERIAL	COLOR	MORDANT	FIBER	PART USED

*Curry powder (Mixture of various spices)

	COLOR	MORDANT	FIBER	PART USED
	bright gold	alum	wool	powder

NOTES _____

_____

*Cutch (gum catechu), *Acacia catechu* or *Uncaria gambier; Acacia* species

	brown	copper	wool	extract
	dark brown	alum	wool	extract

NOTES _____

_____

*Dandelion, *Taraxacum officinale*

	yellow/green	chrome	wool	flowers (fresh)
	yellow	alum	wool	flowers (fresh)
	orange-brown	alum	wool	root
	dark khaki	copper	wool	root

NOTES _____

_____

*Dock, *Rumex* species

	beige	alum	wool	stems and leaves
	medium brown	alum	wool	seeds (ripe)
	gold	alum	wool	seeds (ripe)
	yellow	alum	wool	roots/leaves
	orange	tin	wool	roots
	green	chrome	wool	leaves (fresh)

NOTES _____

_____

Elder, *Sambucus canadensis*

	bluish gray	alum	wool	berries
	blues	chrome	wool	berries

THE BASIC DYEPLANT CHART (CONT'D)

DYE MATERIAL	COLOR	MORDANT	FIBER	PART USED
Elder (cont'd)				
	pinkish beige	alum	wool	berries
	purple	alum	wool	berries
	purple	chrome	wool	berries
	yellow	alum	wool	leaves (fresh)
	green	alum+iron	wool	leaves (fresh)
	pink-violet	alum+vinegar	wool	berries
NOTES	_____			_____
	_____			_____
Fennel, *Foeniculum vulgare*				
	mustard yellow	alum	wool	flowers, leaves
	golden brown	chrome	wool	flowers, leaves
	bright yellow	alum	wool	whole plant
	gold	chrome	wool	whole plant
NOTES	_____			_____
	_____			_____
Feverfew, *Chrysanthemum parthenium*				
	greenish yellow	chrome	wool	leaves/stems
NOTES	_____			_____
	_____			_____
Foxglove, *Digitalis purpurea*				
	chartreuse	alum	wool	flowers
NOTES	_____			_____
	_____			_____
*Fustic (old), *Chlorophora tinctoria* or *Morus tinctoria*				
	bright yellow	chrome	wool	extract
	yellow	alum	wool	extract

THE BASIC DYEPLANT CHART (CONT'D)

DYE MATERIAL	COLOR	MORDANT	FIBER	PART USED
*Fustic (old) (cont'd)				
	green	alum+iron	wool	extract
	bright yellow-green	copper	wool	extract
NOTES				
*Goldenrod, *Solidago* species				
	yellowish green	iron	wool	whole plant
	olive green	iron	wool	whole plant
	avocado green	iron	wool	whole plant
	bright yellow	alum	wool	flowers (fresh)
	rusty orange	chrome	wool	flowers (fresh)
	yellow	alum	wool	leaves/stems
NOTES				
Grapes, *Vitis* species				
	lavender	alum	wool	fruit
	purple	alum	wool	fruit
NOTES				
*Henna, *Lawsonia inermis*				
	yellow	none	wool	powder
	golden yellow	alum	wool	powder
	orange	tin	wool	powder
	golden brown	alum	wool fabric	powder
NOTES				
Holly grape, *Mahonia* species				
	greenish yellow	alum	wool	leaves/stems
NOTES				

THE BASIC DYEPLANT CHART (CONT'D)

DYE MATERIAL	COLOR	MORDANT	FIBER	PART USED
*Hops, *Humulus lupulus*				
	creamy yellow	alum	wool	dried cones
	greenish yellow	chrome	wool	dried cones
	light maize	alum	wool fabric	dried cones
NOTES				
*Indigo, *Indigofera* species				
	blues	(see pages 74–75 and 89–90 for further information)		
Ironweed, *Vernonia* species				
	tan	alum	wool	whole plant
NOTES				
*Joe-Pye-weed, *Eupatorium purpureum*				
	yellow	alum	wool	whole plant
NOTES				
*Koa, *Acacia koa*				
	brown	alum	wool	extract
	tan	none	wool	extract
NOTES				
*Logwood, *Haematoxylum campechianum*				
	blue	alum+vinegar	wool	sawdust
	purple	alum	wool	sawdust

THE BASIC DYEPLANT CHART (CONT'D)

DYE MATERIAL	COLOR	MORDANT	FIBER	PART USED
*Logwood (cont'd)				
	purple	alum+tannin	cotton	sawdust
	dusty purple	alum	wool fabric	sawdust
NOTES	_____			
	_____			
Madder, *Rubia tinctorum*				
	red	alum	wool, silk, mohair	roots
	light red	alum	linen, cotton	roots
	bright red	tin	wool, silk	roots
	light bright red	tin	cotton, linen	roots
	orange	tin	wool	roots
	brown	iron	wool	roots
	reddish purple	chrome	wool	roots
	dark melon	alum+tannin	basketry splint	roots
NOTES	_____			
	_____			
*Marigold, *Tagetes* species				
	yellow-orange	alum+tin	wool	flowers
	gold	alum	wool	flowers
	yellow	alum (bath #2)	wool	flowers
	dull green	alum+iron	wool	flowers
	golden yellow	chrome	wool	flowers
	rust	chrome	wool	flowers
	orange	chrome	wool	flowers
	gold	tin	wool/cotton	flowers
NOTES	_____			
	_____			
Marjoram (sweet), *Origanum majorana*				
	green	alum	wool	whole tops
	olive green	chrome	wool	whole tops
NOTES	_____			
	_____			

DYE MATERIAL	COLOR	MORDANT	FIBER	PART USED
*Milkweed, *Asclepias* species				
	moss green	alum	wool	leaves/flowers
	brassy green	chrome+copper	wool	leaves/flowers
NOTES				
*Mint, *Mentha* species				
	yellow	alum	wool	leaves and stems
	dark gold	chrome	wool	leaves and stems
	yellowish green	none	paper pulp	leaves
NOTES				
Mugwort, *Artemisia* species				
	yellow-green	alum	wool	whole plant
	gold	chrome	wool	whole plant
	soft green	copper	wool	whole plant
	khaki	iron	wool	whole plant
NOTES				
Mulberry, *Morus* species				
	purple	alum	wool	berries
	blue	alum+ammonia	wool	berries
NOTES				
*Mullein (flannel plant, candlewick plant, velvet plant), *Verbascum thapsus* or *V. blattaria*				
	yellow	alum	wool/silk	leaves/stalks
	gold	chrome	wool/silk	leaves/stalks
	bright yellow	alum+tin	wool/silk	leaves/stalks

THE BASIC DYEPLANT CHART (CONT'D)

DYE MATERIAL	COLOR	MORDANT	FIBER	PART USED
*Mullein (cont'd)				
	moss green	alum	wool	leaves/flowers
	dark yellow-green	chrome	wool	leaves/flowers
NOTES				
*Mustard (wild), *Brassica* species				
	bright yellow	alum	wool	flowers
NOTES				
Nettle (stinging), *Urtica dioica*				
	yellow	alum	wool	whole plant
	green	alum+iron	wool	whole plant
	dull gold	alum	wool	flowers
	greenish yellow	alum	wool	tops (fresh)
	beige	alum	wool	leaves/stems
NOTES				
*Oak, *Quercus* species				
	tan	chrome	wool	acorns
	dark brown	iron	wool	acorns
	golden brown	chrome	wool	acorns
	brown	none	wool	bark
	purplish brown	iron	wool	bark
	tan	alum	wool	acorns
	orange	tin	silk	bark
	brown	none	wool	galls
NOTES				
*Onion, *Allium cepa*				
	burnt umber	alum+tannin	cotton embroidery floss	skins

THE BASIC DYEPLANT CHART (CONT'D)

DYE MATERIAL	COLOR	MORDANT	FIBER	PART USED
*Onion (cont'd)				
	lime green	alum	DMC needlepoint wools	skins (purple)
	dull yellow	alum	wool	skins
	orange	alum	wool	skins
	yellow	chrome	wool	skins
	ginger brown	chrome	wool	skins
	golden yellow	copper	wool	skins
	bright golden yellow	tin	wool	skins
	yellow-brown	alum+iron	wool	skins
	yellow-brown	alum+iron	cotton	skins
	tan-orange	alum+tin	wool, cotton, jute	skins
	olive green	alum+tin	wool, cotton	skins (red)
	reddish brown	alum	wool	skins (red)
	reddish brown	chrome	wool	skins (red)
	orange-brown	copper	wool	skins (red)
	dark red-brown	tin	wool	skins (red)
	bronze	alum	wool fabric	skins (mixed)
	soft yellow	alum+tannin	cotton fabric	skins
	yellow-green	alum	wool	whole onions
NOTES				

DYE MATERIAL	COLOR	MORDANT	FIBER	PART USED
*Osage orange (Hedge apple, bois d'arc, horse apple), *Maclura pomifera*				
	bright yellow	alum	wool	extract
	yellow	tin	wool	extract
	gold	chrome	wool	extract
	light yellow	alum+tannin	basketry splint	extract
NOTES				

DYE MATERIAL	COLOR	MORDANT	FIBER	PART USED
Pear, *Pyrus communis*				
	yellows	alum	wool	leaves
NOTES				

THE BASIC DYEPLANT CHART (CONT'D)

DYE MATERIAL	COLOR	MORDANT	FIBER	PART USED

Plum, *Prunus domestica*

	brown	alum	wool	bark

NOTES _____

_____

Pokeweed (pokeberry, pigeonberry, pokan, coakum, inkberry), *Phytolacca americana*

	red	alum	wool or silk	berries
	pink	alum	cotton or linen	berries
	yellowish red	tin	wool or silk	berries
	shades of pink	tin	cotton or linen	berries
	rusty red	chrome	wool	berries

NOTES _____

_____

*Queen-Anne's-lace (wild carrot), *Daucus carota*

	pale yellow	alum	wool	flowers/stems
	tan	chrome	wool	flowers/stems

NOTES _____

_____

Rhubarb, *Rheum rhabarbarum*

	bright orange	tin	wool	leaves (tops)
	rusty brown	tin	wool	leaves (tops)

NOTES _____

_____

*Rosemary, *Rosmarinus officinalis*

	yellow-green	alum	wool	leaves/flowers

NOTES _____

_____

THE BASIC DYEPLANT CHART (CONT'D)

DYE MATERIAL	COLOR	MORDANT	FIBER	PART USED
Safflower (false saffron, bastard saffron, American saffron, dyer's thistle), *Carthamus tinctorius*				
	bright yellow	alum	wool or silk	flowers
	rusty red	tin	wool or silk	flowers
	dusty rose	alum	wool or silk	flowers
	orange	tin	silk	flowers
NOTES				
Sage, *Salvia officinalis*				
	yellow ochre	alum	wool	leaves and stems
	yellow ochre	chrome	wool	leaves and stems
	yellow ochre	copper	wool	leaves and stems
	lemon yellow	tin	wool	leaves and stems
	greenish gray	iron	wool	leaves and stems
NOTES				
St.-John's-wort, *Hypericum perforatum*				
	yellow	alum	wool	tops
NOTES				
***Sorrel,** *Rumex acetosa*				
	yellow	alum	wool	whole plant
	pink	chrome	wool	root
NOTES				
***Sumac,** *Rhus glabra*				
	black	iron	wool	berries/leaves
	yellow	alum	wool	extract
	tan	alum	wool	berries/leaves

THE BASIC DYEPLANT CHART (CONT'D)

DYE MATERIAL	COLOR	MORDANT	FIBER	PART USED
*Sumac (cont'd)				
	green	copper	wool	berries/leaves
	tan	alum+tannin	basketry splint	extract
NOTES				
*Sunflower, *Helianthus annuus* or *H. maximiliani*				
	yellow-gold	alum+chrome	wool	flowers
	yellow	alum	wool	seeds
	orange-yellow	alum+ammonia	wool	flowers
	olive brown	alum+copper	wool	flowers
NOTES				
Sweet woodruff, *Asperula odorata*				
	tan	alum	wool	stems/leaves
	red	alum	wool	roots
NOTES				
*Tansy, *Tanacetum vulgare*				
	yellow-green	alum	wool	young leaves
	greenish yellow	alum	wool	flowers
	yellow	alum	wool	flowers
	strong yellow	alum	wool	flowers
	dark green	iron	wool	tops
	brown	tin	wool	flowers
NOTES				
*Tea, *Thea sinensis*				
	dark tan	none	raffia	leaves
	tan	alum+vinegar	wool	leaves

THE BASIC DYEPLANT CHART (CONT'D)

DYE MATERIAL	COLOR	MORDANT	FIBER	PART USED
*Tea (cont'd)				
	tan	alum	cotton fabric	leaves
	medium brown	chrome	wool	leaves
	grayish tan	iron	wool	leaves
	greenish brown	alum+iron	wool	leaves
NOTES				
Thyme, *Thymus vulgaris*				
	grayish gold	alum	wool	leaves (in fall)
	yellow	tin	wool	leaves (in fall)
	gold	tin+ammonia	wool	leaves (in fall)
	bronze	alum+copper	wool	leaves (in fall)
NOTES				
Toadflax (butter-and-eggs, yellow toadflax, wild snapdragon), *Linaria vulgaris*				
	yellow-green	alum+copper	wool	whole plant
	yellow	alum	wool	flowers
	chartreuse	tin	wool	whole plant
NOTES				
*Tomato, *Lycopersicon lycopersicum*				
	reddish brown	none	wool/silk	vine
	light yellow	alum	wool/silk	vine
	brown	alum	wool	leaves
NOTES				
*Turmeric, *Curcuma domestica*				
	bright yellow	alum	cornhusks	powdered spice
	golden orange	alum+vinegar	wool	powdered spice

THE BASIC DYEPLANT CHART (CONT'D)

DYE MATERIAL	COLOR	MORDANT	FIBER	PART USED
*Turmeric (cont'd)				
	bright yellow	alum+tannin	cotton embroidery floss	powdered spice
	bright yellow-gold	none	cotton fabric	powdered spice
	bright gold	none	wool fabric	powdered spice
	bright yellow	alum+tannin	basketry splint	powdered spice
NOTES	_____			
	_____			
Weld, *Reseda luteola*				
	yellow	alum	wool/cotton	whole plant/leaves
NOTES	_____			
	_____			
*Woad (asp of Jerusalem), *Isatis tinctoria*				
	blue	none	wool	young leaves
	pink	alum	wool	young leaves
NOTES	_____			
	_____			
*Yarrow (milfoil, thousand seal), *Achillea millefolium*				
	yellow	alum	wool	flowers
	olive green	iron	wool	all parts
	green	copper	wool	leaves
	brilliant yellow	tin	wool	whole plant
	yellow-gray	iron	wool	whole plant
NOTES	_____			
	_____			

☗ chapter 2 ☗

Preparation for Dyeing

*t**he wonderful thing** about natural dyeing is that you can do it yourself in your own home, using inexpensive and easy-to-find equipment. The whole process of natural dyeing involves only five basic steps:

Step 1. Gather, grow, or buy the dyestuffs. Colors for dyeing can be found in flowers, herbs, vegetables, roots, leaves, berries, and barks. You can either gather them from the wild or grow them in your own garden. Some colors, such as cochineal, are even found in insects.

Step 2. Prepare the fiber or fabric by washing or scouring it.

Step 3. Mordant the fiber or the fabric with a chemical that helps it absorb the dyes.

Step 4. Make the dyebath or heat the dyestuff to extract the color.

Step 5. Dye the fiber in the prepared dyebath.

Natural dyeing does not have to be a complicated process. As in any craft, the more experienced you become, the more you want to explore and experiment. In the beginning, however, following these five steps allows you to produce more than enough colors for your weaving, spinning, knitting, rugmaking, quilting, embroidery, or needlework projects!

Equipment and Supplies

You can have fun with natural dyes without a great financial commitment. As a matter of fact, when you are a beginner, most of the equipment that you need is household kitchen utensils that you may already have on hand or that you can pick up inexpensively at garage sales or thrift stores — they do not have to be new to be useful. I bought several pots and pans (even a lot of natural fiber yarns) at the local Goodwill Store for only a few dollars. You don't need all of these items for your first dyeing projects, but they all come in handy sooner or later. Just add to your collection as you go. In addition to the following, the only other things required are a heat source of some

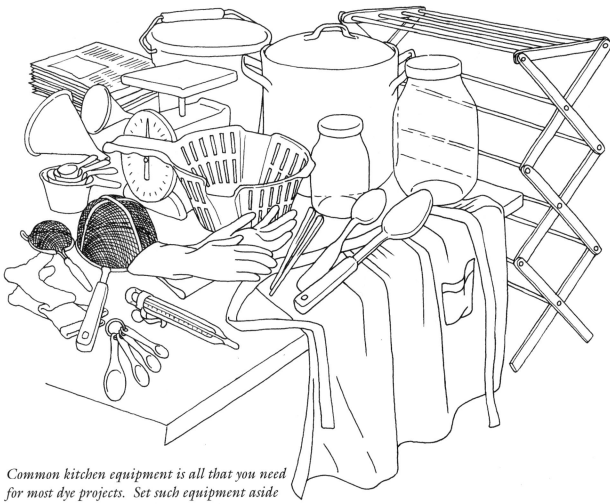

*Common kitchen equipment is all that you need for most dye projects. Set such equipment aside **only** for dyeing and no other purpose.*

kind (a hot plate will do) and running water.

Timer. I use the timer on my microwave oven.

Stirring rods or spoons. These should be of nonreactive metal, stainless steel, or glass. I use old wooden chopsticks. I mark my chopstick dye stirrers with permanent marker and use them over and over for the same mordants and dyes. You can buy packages of these at Oriental foods or import stores. Wooden dowels or even clean twigs or sticks also work.

Rubber or vinyl gloves. I buy gloves by the boxful at the drugstore and dispose of them after using.

A place to hang yarns and fabrics while drying. This may not seem very important until you have five or six skeins of dripping wet yarn and no place to put them. I use a folding wooden clothesdrying rack that I bought at K-Mart for $10.00. I hang yarns on it with paper clips bent into S hooks and simply drape fabrics across the bars. You can place the rack in a garage or even on top of a stack of newspapers in a bathtub to drip until dry.

Nonreactive pots and pans with lids. You need pots and pans made of stainless steel or enamel (with no chips) in various sizes. I use two 5-gallon enamel canning pots for most of my fabric dyeing projects and several smaller pots for the yarns. Smaller pots are adequate for most purposes unless you are dyeing several pounds of yarn at a time, in which case you need a 5-gallon pot. (A practical note — I find it disconcerting to use black pots because I can't tell by looking into them what colors my plants have rendered. The next time I shop for dyepots, I'll buy white or cream-colored ones.)

Old knee-high hose. I use these to hold small amounts of raw fibers, such as cotton embroidery flosses. Make sure that the hose are old and well-washed: The hose have often been dyed "skin colors" and can ruin the dyebath if any color is left in them.

Scale. Use a small postal or diet scale for only a few ounces of yarn. My husband has a wonderful, fancy scale for beermaking that I "borrow." Although one of this type is not necessary, it does come in handy for weighing several pounds of fabric or yarns at once.

Old jars with lids. Gallon jars are used for the indigo vat described on pages 89–90. Other jars are useful for mixing or storing dyes.

Plastic colander.

Measuring spoons and cups. Either plastic or stainless steel is fine.

Large, heatproof glass measuring cup.

Cooking thermometer. A simple candy thermometer works.

Plastic dishpan or bucket. This is used for soaking yarns and fibers.

A smock or apron. This is handy to protect your clothes from splashes and spills — and there will be plenty!

Old newspapers. Be sure to protect the floor and countertops of your workspace.

Stainless steel strainers of various sizes. Old tea strainers come in handy.

Litmus paper. For greater accuracy, test the pH balance of your water.

Plastic buckets.

Funnels of various sizes. Don't use aluminum.

Optional: Old iron, tin, aluminum, or copper pots. Early methods of dyeing relied on the pot that the yarn was dyed in to produce the mordanting effect. Although it is romantic to picture steaming black iron cauldrons or shiny copper kettles hanging above outdoor fires or large fireplaces, they are impractical for modern use. They are fun to have for experiments, but it is impossible to control the amount of metal salts released from these pots into the dyebath.

Safety Precautions

Never use your dye equipment or supplies for food preparation. Most mordants are dangerous chemicals that can leave poisonous residues in the dyepots. For safety reasons, have a set of pots, pans, stirring implements, and so on to be used only for dyeing. Label them prominently and store them away from curious children and unwary adults.

Many of the chemicals and assistants used in natural dyeing can be dangerous if improperly used. Repeated, unprotected exposure to chemicals can gradually sensitize the dyer until an allergy or more severe problem develops. For example, chrome (potassium dichromate) and copper (copper sulfate) are extremely toxic and may be fatal if eaten.

Keeping Good Records

For future reference, it's always a good idea to keep a record of your dye activities. At the very least, you should make a note of dyestuff used, time and place of collection, mordant used, fiber content of yarn or fabric, yarn or fabric supplier, and date. Be sure to attach a small sample of the yarn (and the tag from purchased skeins) to your notes. In addition to being a record of the project, this will also help you remember which experiments you have or have not tried. Take notes as you work; don't rely on memory to reconstruct them later. Believe me,

Safety Rules for Dyers

◆ **Always wear rubber gloves.** Even alum and cream of tartar can be rough on your hands.

◆ **Do your dyeing outside** or have a lot of ventilation if you must dye inside.

◆ **Wipe up spills promptly.**

I use old disposable rags or paper towels for this purpose. This is especially important when using mordants such as copper or chrome.

◆ **Always add the chemicals to the water,** and not the water to the chemicals — there is less danger of adverse chemical reactions, such as fizzing or splashing.

◆ **Always store mordants, dyes, and dye equipment in a safe place.** Make sure they are labelled and put away out of the reach of curious children and pets.

◆ **Always keep the pots covered** while dyeing or mordanting. Avoid inhaling fumes. If you leave the pots for longer than a few hours, you may wish to secure the lids, especially if you have pets or small children.

◆ **Do not eat or drink while mordanting.** It is too easy to pick up the wrong container and take a drink from it when you are preoccupied with your work. In a college painting class, I

once picked up a cup of turpentine by mistake and took a sip of it, thinking it was a soft drink. Sometimes you learn your lessons the hard way!

---

after dyeing twenty skeins of yarn in different colors, you won't remember what you did or did not do to produce those luscious colors!

Here are some other details that make your records more helpful to you in the future:

Part of the plant used (fruit, pods, leaves, stems, roots, whole plant, and so on)
Quantity of plant material used
Type of water used (distilled, tap, rain, or river water)
Mordanting process used
Length of time mordanted
Which assistants added to the bath (vinegar, cream of tartar, soap, ammonia)

Proportion of dyestuff to fiber used
Temperature of the dyebath
Testing of fiber for lightfastness or washfastness
Pressed specimen of the dyeplant or a photograph or a drawing of the plant, along with notes about it.

Dye records can be as elaborate or as simple as you wish. Keep them in a loose-leaf notebook (see sample form on page 32), on file cards, or in file folders. I like to use a loose-leaf notebook system because I can line up the yarns next to one another and then remove the pages and lay them next to each other in order to compare the colors.

DATE:_____

DYE PLANT:_____

    TIME AND PLACE COLLECTED:_____

    PART OF PLANT USED:_____

    QUANTITY USED:_____

YARN/FABRIC FIBER CONTENT:_____

    SUPPLIER:_____

PROPORTION OF DYESTUFF TO FIBER:_____

MORDANT:_____ ASSISTANTS:_____

    PROCESS:_____

    LENGTH OF TIME MORDANTED:_____

WATER:_____ WATER TEMPERATURE:_____

LIGHTFASTNESS:_____ WASHFASTNESS:_____

NOTES:_____

_____

_____

SAMPLE OF DYEPLANT:

SAMPLE OF YARN/FABRIC:

Labels for Your Yarns

Label your skeins, so that you can later identify exactly what you did to a yarn to get a specific color. Some dyers tie a system of knots into the strings that they use to keep the yarns from tangling. One knot could mean that the yarn was mordanted with alum; two knots could mean that chrome was used, and so on. One dyer uses a series of buttons tied to the skeins. Another ties different types of twine and string to her yarns. I find it less confusing to cut small squares of plastic from discarded milk jugs, mark them with a permanent marker, and tie them onto the larger skeins. While the yarns are drying, I hang the tag from a paper clip and use the clip to hold the skein to my drying rack. Later, I attach more permanent labels.

For embroidery cottons and small skeins of needlepoint yarns, I number the skein holders and list the information about that particular color on a separate sheet of paper. Because these yarns and threads get used up fairly rapidly, I make sure to save a snippet of each skein for my record book.

Plastic tag labelled with mordant used on this ready-to-dye skein of yarn.

Dyeing Natural Fibers with Natural Dyes

Many people are surprised to find that you can dye not only wool yarn but also cotton or wool fabrics, as well as embroidery flosses, linens, silks, and even basketry fibers with natural dyes. As a matter of fact, all natural fibers can be dyed with natural dyes. The protein fibers, such as wool or silk, dye easily. The plant, or vegetable, fibers, such as cotton, linen, jute, sisal, raffia, and so on, can also be dyed with natural dyes, but it takes a bit more work. This book covers only the dyeing of natural fibers in all forms — raw fibers, yarns, threads, and fabrics.

Many manufacturers and fiber suppliers now offer natural, untreated yarns, fabrics, and raw fibers that are ideal for dyeing. Some suppliers that I heartily recommend are listed in the Appendix.

The preparation process is not the same for all of the fibers, but none is exceptionally difficult.

Preparation of Wools for Dyeing

Wool yarns are packaged in a variety of ways, including cones, skeins, tubes, and balls. For dyeing, looped skeins are those easiest to handle. To make skeins, you can use one of the many different kinds of skein winders on the market. For smaller amounts of yarn, a skein winder is not necessary. Simply wind the yarn around two pegs on a warping board, the back of a chair, or even between your fingers and bent elbow. After you have wound the wool into these skeins, tie the two ends of the yarn together in a firm knot.

I sometimes wind small skeins around a piece of flexible cardboard that can be bent to remove the yarn. Skeins of 1 to 6 ounces are easier to handle than larger ones; my skeins tend to weigh about 4 ounces, except for the smaller needlepoint wools and embroidery threads that

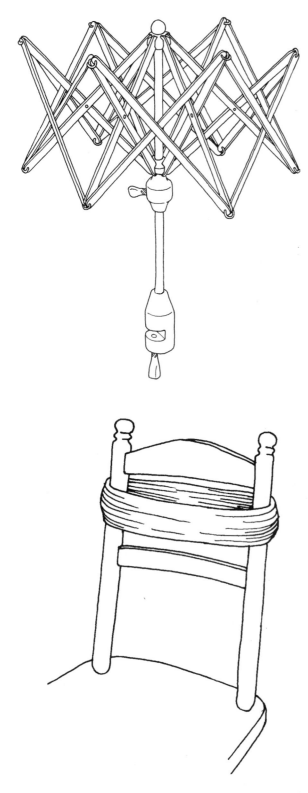

I use. For dye experiments I use even smaller skeins.

With pieces of cotton twine, make loose figure-eight ties at three or four places around the skein of yarn to keep it from tangling. Don't tie string too tightly, or you will have a tie-dyed effect. (This method is sometimes used deliberately to create interesting effects on the yarn).

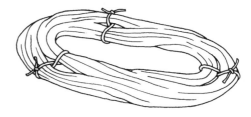

Make loose figure-eight ties at several places around the skein to avoid tangles.

Washing Wool Yarns

If you are using commercial yarns or your own handspun yarns, they should be washed, or *scoured,* before mordanting to remove the lanolin, which is the sheep's natural oil. Scouring also removes the surface soil, synthetic finishes, and other oils and greases from woolens that can hamper the absorption of mordants and dyes and make the color splotchy or mottled. Many of the common problems that occur in dyeing, such as muddy colors or streaking, are directly related to the improper preparation of fibers. It is worth your time to do a thorough job of fiber preparation before mordanting or dyeing to ensure a high-quality dyeing job.

If the yarn is dirty, you may want to do a more thorough job of washing it by using the following method:

1. Make a solution of washing soda and neutral soap in 2 to 3 gallons of water for each pound of yarn scoured.
2. Add the yarn, and heat the solution to about 110° to 120°F. Maintain this temperature for 30 to 60 minutes.

If you use a great deal of yarn, a skein winder (above) is a useful tool, but the back of a chair is a perfectly fine substitute.

3. Remove the yarn, rinse thoroughly (in water of the same temperature) until free of soap, and hang to dry or mordant immediately. Handle the wools gently to avoid shrinking or matting them. Never wring roughly, agitate, or twist the skeins to remove the water.

Scouring Raw Fleece

Many spinners prefer to wash and dye the fleece before spinning it into yarn. Fleece that is dyed before being spun into yarn is known as *dyed-in-the-wool*. Since I usually wash and dye only small amounts of raw fleece at a time for use in felting projects, I place the raw fibers in an old knee-high hose to wash it. Or, I sometimes tie the fleece into small bundles of cheesecloth. If you must scour a larger amount of wool — a whole fleece, for instance — before dyeing and spinning it, this method is not feasible. Although experts disagree on the best way, the consensus is that fleece should be washed in hot water, left to soak for a few hours, and then rinsed in more hot water (or water at about the same temperature as the wash water).

1. Pick out any burrs, grass, and other vegetable matter, and fluff out the fibers by pulling

---

A Hint about Dyeing Fleece

If the wool has been properly sorted and washed before mordanting and dyeing, it has a better chance of being dyed a uniform color. Even with the most careful attention, various parts of the same fleece may react to a dye in different ways. As with all other "accidents," you can use this effect to your advantage. Fleece with splotches or uneven coloring can be carded and spun together with other fleece to produce a heathered or rainbow effect in your handspun yarn. No one will ever know that the yarn was not designed this way in the first place!

---

gently and *teasing* them out with your fingers.

2. Prepare a soapy water bath in a large basin, dishpan, sink, or other container with a neutral soap, such as Ivory Flakes (or see box on page 36), and enough hot water (about 115°F) to cover the fleece. Add the fleece to the water, and push it down in the water to soak. Do not agitate the fleece!

3. Cover the basin, so that the water temperature remains fairly constant. Let the wool soak for several hours. Check to be sure the water does not get cool.

4. Gently squeeze the wool by hand several times and remove it from the water. Squeeze out excess water, but do not wring out or twist the fleece!

5. Again fill the basin with hot water (at about the same temperature as the wash water), add the fleece, and rinse. Gently squeeze the fleece in the water, taking care to avoid agitating it. When the fleece is clean, remove it from the water.

6. Lay the fleece on a towel placed on a stack of newspapers to drain. If the fleece is to be mordanted immediately, it is not necessary for it to dry completely. You can keep it damp in a plastic bag for several days until it can be mordanted or dyed. If you wish to keep it damp, store the fleece in the refrigerator during hot weather, if possible, to prevent mold or mildew.

If you allow the fleece to dry, you must thoroughly wet it again before mordanting or dyeing by soaking it for a few hours or overnight in a bath of warm water. Remove the fleece, drain it, and lay it aside while you are preparing the mordant or dye bath.

Cotton and Other Plant Fibers

Unless cotton and linen yarns or fabrics are ordered from a supplier that specializes in "ready-to-dye" fabrics, they must be washed thoroughly, or *scoured,* before mordanting. Just as wool fibers contain lanolin from the sheep, plant fibers such as cottons or linens contain natural waxes that should be removed before mordanting or dyeing.

Cottons and linens are not nearly as sensitive to heat changes as wool and thus can actually be boiled while scouring, mordanting, or dyeing.

1. Soak the fabrics or yarns thoroughly in hot water.
2. Dissolve a neutral soap in 4 or 5 gallons of hot water (about 140°F). Add 1 ounce of washing soda if the fiber is exceptionally dirty.
3. Wash the material thoroughly and then rinse repeatedly to remove all of the soap. The fiber can now be dried or immediately mordanted and dyed.

Although I have not tried it, one author even suggests that jute or linen skeins can be washed in the washing machine on a gentle cycle. Before you try this, make sure that all skeins are securely tied in three or four places to prevent tangling.

Degumming Silk Yarns and Fabrics

Raw silks contain a large percentage of *sericin* (natural "silk glue"), which must be removed from the fibers before mordanting or dyeing so that the finished yarn or fabric will be lustrous, not dull. Sericin is most commonly removed by boiling the yarn in soapy water. This process is called degumming.

Silk yarns and fabrics can be degummed by using a method similar to the one outlined above for cottons, with a few exceptions.

1. Soak the fabrics or yarns thoroughly in warm water.
2. For 1 pound or less of fiber, mix a solution consisting of 1 ounce of washing soda, mild soap (enough to make low suds), and 4 gallons of water.

A Note About Soaps

Several neutral soaps have recently come on the market that are specifically formulated for washing wool fibers. They are known by various brand names and include Meadows French Lavender Wool Wash, Meadows Fibermaster Ultra Grease & Stain Formula, and Soltec's Lano-Rinse Conditioner for Wool and Lano-Wash Gentle Shampoo for Wool. (For suppliers' addresses, see Appendix.)

3. Add the silk to the pot, bring the water to a boil, turn down the heat, and simmer for about 30 minutes. Make sure to add more water as necessary to maintain the water level.
4. Remove the silk from the water.
5. Repeat steps 2 and 3 above.
6. Remove the silks and cool. Rinse thoroughly with warm water until soap is removed.
7. Mordant immediately or dry at room temperature. If you dry the silk, it must be rewetted thoroughly before it can be mordanted or dyed.

Basketry Fibers — Reed, Raffia, Splint, and Cornhusks

I have found that, in general, basketry fibers like reed, raffia, splint, and cornhusks do not need to be scoured before dyeing. In fact, since these fibers are susceptible to heat damage, the less time they are heated or immersed in hot water the better. I simply soak the materials in warm water until they are well wetted before mordanting them.

On the other hand, jute and sisal dye better after being scoured. Follow the same method as for cotton (pages 35–36).

chapter 3

Mordants
and Mordanting

*M*ordanting is probably* the most misunderstood, confusing, and perhaps intimidating concept for beginning dyers. In reality, the principle is simple: Mordants are simply metallic salts that help the dyes bind to the fibers. The metallic salt fixes onto the fiber, and the dye fixes onto the metal salt. The word *mordant* derives from the Latin *mordere*, which means to bite. Basically, mordants do three things: First, they help dyes bind to the fibers, as already mentioned. Second, they affect the color produced by a dye (for example, onion skins used with alum make an orange/brown color, whereas used with chrome they make a more reddish brown color). Third, mordants work to make and keep the colors lightfast and to brighten the colors.

Dyers have been using mordants for thousands of years and there is good reason why certain mordants are usually used with certain dyes. Once you understand the basics of why a certain mordant or assistant is used with a particular dye, you needn't be tied down to strict recipes, and it becomes easier to make up your own recipes and achieve the colors that you want. Dyers rarely agree on how much of a particular mordant to use. The amounts mentioned here are only suggestions for starting points. It's always better to use too little of a mordant than too much. See the Mordanting Chart on pages 40–41 for further information and for specific precautions to use with the various mordants.

While you are learning the basics of natural dyeing, you can get by with just alum and cream of tartar. Later, you can try chrome, iron, copper, or tin to get different colors and effects. The Baby's First Garden blanket (pages 125 and 99–101) was dyed using only alum-mordanted yarns with cream of tartar, baking soda, and vinegar added as assistants. As you can see, this gave me plenty of color choices.

Mordants through the Ages

Dyers haven't always been able to send off an order to their favorite mail-order supplier or to call a toll-free number with credit card in hand to get their needed supply of mordants. Early American colonists, for instance, used whatever was nearby — usually salt, vinegar, cream of tartar, or soda from the general store, iron filings from the village blacksmith's shop, and "drip lye" or "chamber lye." Drip lye was homemade from wood ashes, and chamber lye was urine (a common source of various salts and ammonia). When tannin was used as a mordant, it was gathered from oak, hemlock, or sumac galls and leaves. Sorrel was used for its oxalic acid content.

Navajo women traditionally mordanted with ashes from burned juniper branches mixed with water, as well as with staghorn mosses and various lichens. Wood ashes have also been used as mordanting agents in South America. The Ojibway used naturally occurring materials for mordants — wood ashes, rusty water, local clays, and grindstone dust. In Bali, coconut palm leaves were burned and mixed with water and used as mordants. A mixture of sheep manure and water is a traditional mordant in many different cultures.

Historically, dyers often used metal pots that acted as mordants for the yarns, and some of the more traditionally oriented dyers still use aluminum, iron, copper, or tin pots. Just for fun, you may want to try this method of mordanting. The problem with using pots as mordants, however, is that the amount of metal salts released cannot be controlled. It can be safer, however. Using a copper pot, for example, is safer than using the pure metallic salt, which is extremely toxic.

The Mordants

The most common mordants are alum, iron, tin, copper, and chrome. Unless you live near a large chemical supplier that sells in smaller quantities, I suggest that you order these items from mail-order suppliers (see Appendix for addresses.) Austin, Texas, where I live, is the home of a large university and several small colleges, but even here I can't get supplies locally. Most local suppliers sell chemicals like tin only in 1-pound quantities or larger (and tin costs more than $300.00 per pound!). Alum and other assistants may be available in a large pharmacy or grocery store.

I use alum and cream of tartar alone 95 percent of the time with a variety of other assistants used in small quantities to make color changes. Although I don't have small children at my house, I am concerned about the possible long-term health effects of using the more poisonous chemicals. I use the other mordants only now and then as a matter of curiosity.

Alum (potassium aluminum sulfate). A white mineral deposit found in many types of rock formations in various parts of the world, alum is sold in both powdered form or granules. Southwestern Indians have traditionally used a native alum caused by water evaporation that is found as a deposit around aluminum-bearing rocks. Alum is the mordant most often used by natural dyers. It tends to set the colors, although it does not change them. Pickling alum (ammonium alum) can be used, if necessary, but it is not as effective as potassium aluminum sulfate. Mordanting with alum sometimes slightly yellows the yarn or fabric: This is normal. Too much alum in the pot makes wool feel sticky.

Alum-mordanted wool stores well whether wet or dry. Alum is relatively nontoxic, but it is very astringent and drying to the skin, so wear gloves while using it.

Chrome (potassium dichromate). A bright orange chemical that is very sensitive to light, chrome should be stored in a dark place and kept covered. The mordanting or dyeing pot should also be covered when using chrome or the yarns will turn green. In the dyebath, chrome enhances shades of brass, warm brown colors, or gold. This chemical is very caustic and poisonous in all forms (as a dry chemical, in a liquid solution, or as fumes). Use outdoors or with plenty of ventilation. Be sure to wear rubber gloves and clean up any splashes immediately. If you decide to use chrome in your dyeing, set one pot aside for chrome use only. Mark the chrome container well, and keep it out of the reach of children or pets. Chrome is usually used in small quantities, so you won't need much of this chemical.

Chrome is most effective when used as a mordant before dyeing the yarn. This lessens the time that the chrome might be exposed to light. (See pages 45–47 for information on premordanting.)

Copper (copper sulfate). Also known as blue vitriol, copper is a very pretty, deep turquoise color. It is a poisonous chemical, however, sometimes used by plumbers to kill tree roots that clog sewer pipes. Copper usually has a slight greening effect when used in dyeing. Copper can be used alone as a mordant or as a postmordant additive to *sadden* (darken) colors or turn a yellow or a yellow-green color to a more definite green. A small amount of this chemical also goes a long way — 3 ounces will mordant about 3 to 4 pounds of wool. Copper works well with wools but not on plant fibers or silks.

Iron (ferrous sulfate). Also known as green vitriol or copperas, iron saddens colors, bringing out green shades. I usually add iron at the end of a dyebath to change existing colors rather than use it alone as a mordant. Too much iron makes wool hard or brittle. Iron works well on wool and some plant fibers but should never be used on silk because of its harshness. Iron can sometimes be found in garden supply stores; ask for pure ferrous sulfate with no additives.

Dyers who seek dull, sad colors often prefer to overdye naturally gray or silver wools instead of using iron, which is potentially damaging to

fine fibers.

Tannin (tannic acid). A natural substance found in tree barks, oak galls, sumac, tea leaves, and other plant parts, tannic acid is usually used as an assistant with alum for dyeing cotton. (See Dye Assistants and Additives below.) Tannic acid can also be used alone as a mordant for wool to make tan or brown colors. Wool premordanted with tannin before dyeing tends to darken with age.

Tin (stannous chloride). Tin should be stored in a tightly closed container in a relatively cool place out of the reach of children or pets. This is used in very small amounts; 3 ounces lasts a long time and mordants about 5 pounds of wool. Too much tin makes wool brittle and harsh to the touch. It is best used as a postmordant to *bloom* (brighten) colors. Tin is not as effective on plant fibers such as cotton or linen.

Dye Assistants and Additives

Assistants are not mordants but are useful substances that help the yarns absorb the dyes more evenly. Additives are usually added in small amounts during either the mordanting or the dyeing process. To bring about a change of color, I use just a pinch of cream of tartar or a few drops of household ammonia or vinegar to 1 ounce of wool. Some other commonly used assistants include baking soda, Glauber's salt, plain salt, tannin, and washing soda.

MORDANTING CHART

The chart that follows is a basic guide to mordants, assistants, and their characteristics, with special notes on their uses. Study this chart to get an understanding of the various ways that the mordants change the colors of the dyes and generally affect fibers. Each mordant gives natural fibers an underlying tint, so that even fibers dyed with different colors tend to harmonize with each other when they have been treated with the same mordant.

COMMON NAME	SCIENTIFIC NAME	EFFECT	USED FOR
Alum	Potassium aluminum sulfate	Brightens colors; makes colors more lightfast and washfast; slight yellowing effect on some colors	Pre-, simultaneous, or postmordanting
Chrome	Potassium dichromate	Darkens colors slightly; softens the texture of wools; has a browning effect	Lightfastness; washfastness; premordanting most effective
Copper	Copper sulfate	Greening effect overall; as a mordant, turns yarn bluish	Postmordanting usually; premordanting also
Iron	Ferrous sulfate	Dulls or "saddens" colors	Postmordanting
Tannin	Tannic acid		Assistant with alum on cottons; premordanting on wools
Tin	Stannous chloride	Brightens most colors; brassy effects	Postmordanting

ENHANCES WHAT COLORS	HOW MUCH TO USE? (PER POUND OF FIBER)	SPECIAL NOTES	SAFETY PRECAUTIONS
All	2–4 ounces (4 tablespoons) + 1 ounce (2 tablespoons) cream of tartar	Too much makes wool sticky and harsh; easiest to use	Causes nausea if eaten; highly astringent; dries skin
Alters yellows and oranges to golds and browns; brings out reds and oranges; "blooms" colors	½ ounce (3 tablespoons) + 1 ounce cream of tartar	Too much overly darkens or dulls colors; highly sensitive to light; keep pots covered; dry away from light; store undyed wool in dark place	Extremely poisonous; skin irritant; wear rubber gloves; avoid fumes; most dangerous mordant
Greens	2 tablespoons		Extremely poisonous
Blacks	2 tablespoons	Too much hardens wool; may darken on exposure to light	Poisonous in amounts necessary for mordanting
Tans and browns	1 ounce		Tends to darken with age if used as premordant
Brightens yellows, reds, and oranges; "blooms" colors	2 teaspoons per pound + 1–2 ounces cream of tartar	Too much makes wool brittle and harsh	Harsh to skin; poisonous in amounts necessary for mordanting

Ammonia. This is sometimes used as an afterbath to intensify reds, blues, or yellows. Use the clear, nondetergent type to make the dyebath more alkaline. Ammonia can be purchased at a pharmacy or grocery store, although the nonsudsy type may be more readily found at a hardware store or large discount chain store.

Baking soda. Bicarbonate of soda is inexpensive and easy to find in grocery stores in the baking section. Used as an afterbath or as an additive, baking soda, which is an alkali, can sometimes turn a violet or purple dye, such as logwood, to a more bluish color.

Cream of tartar (tartaric acid). The same fine, white powder often used in baking, cream of tartar is sometimes used in the dyebath along with alum (and sometimes with tin) to keep wool soft. It also evens out and may brighten colors (especially reds and yellows), and it makes colors faster by assisting the mordant in binding to the fibers. It also helps protect wools from mordant damage such as brittleness or harshness. Cream of tartar is nontoxic and is easy to find in grocery stores among the baking supplies. I like to buy it in bulk at a local natural foods store, since it's less expensive this way and I use quite a lot of it.

Glauber's salt (sodium sulfate). Glauber's salt slows down the absorption of dyes into wool fibers and speeds up absorption of the dyes into cotton. Glauber's salt is thus a "leveling agent" on either fiber, preventing streaking and helping to exhaust the color from the dyebath. Glauber's salt also improves washfastness with certain dyes, especially cochineal. To use, dissolve ½ cup Glauber's salt in 1 pint of hot water. Halfway through the dyeing process, remove the fiber and stir in the solution, mixing well. Replace the fiber and continue dyeing.

Glauber's salt is also useful to make a match of two slightly different shaded skeins of wool that have been dyed with the same plant. For 1 pound of wool, dissolve 1 cup Glauber's salt in hot water, and add to 1 gallon of warm water (the water should cover the wool.) Stir to mix well. Add the two skeins of wetted wool to the bath and simmer for about 30 minutes, or until the skeins are a better match. Let the yarn cool in the dyebath, remove, and rinse.

Salt (plain). Add plain table salt to the dyebath or use it as an afterbath. Salt intensifies colors and helps wool absorb dyes evenly. It is especially effective in a cold-water rinse on cotton fabrics to help make the dyes fast.

Vinegar (diluted acetic acid). Use vinegar to help set colors after dyeing. You can also use it with berry dyes to bring out color or change violet or purple colors to a more reddish hue. Plain white vinegar is preferable to other types (except, see page 143).

Tannin (tannic acid) is a light brown powder that is used along with alum as an assistant on cotton fabrics and threads. Tannic acid is found naturally in oak galls, nuts, various tree barks, and sumac plants. Some dyestuffs already contain tannin (tea, for example) and thus do not require a separate mordant. Mordants can be added, however, if you wish to produce additional color changes. Tannic acid sometimes darkens colors.

Washing soda or sal soda (sodium carbonate). Another alkali, washing soda is used to scour some fibers and in conjunction with some indigo recipes.

Sodium benzoate. This chemical may be used as a preservative to avoid the formation of mold on dyebaths that you might wish to store.

The addition and use of these assistants may seem like extra work and expense, but their importance becomes clear when you realize that natural dyeing is a chemical reaction or process. Mordants, coloring matter in the plant materials, minerals present in your water supply, and assistants all work together to form a chemical reaction that makes the beautiful colors of natural dyes.

Mordanting Natural Fibers

My mordanting (and dyeing) procedures are, for the most part, based loosely on methods used by Anne Bliss and documented in her books as well as in an article printed in *Shuttle, Spindle & Dyepot* magazine (see Suggested Reading, page 150). I do not follow separate, strict recipes for individual dye plants. Instead, I have formulated some basic guidelines that I use for all plants. Even these instructions and amounts are not set in stone; they can be changed according to the whim and inspiration of the dyer. However, I have found them to be good basic guidelines that can be changed according to the season and the amount of dye material and time that I have available.

Presoaking the Fibers

All fibers, whether raw, spun into yarns, or woven into fabrics, have to be thoroughly wetted before mordanting or dyeing begins. Many problems with the absorption of dyes into fabrics are caused by improper wetting before dyeing. Thorough wetting can sometimes be accomplished only by soaking the item for hours in warm or hot water. Some fibers, such as basketry splint, take several hours to absorb enough water to become sufficiently wet. Others, such as thin, ready-to-be dyed cotton fabrics, take only 30 to 40 minutes. Sometimes you can tell by looking at a fabric closely whether it has absorbed enough water or not. In general, when the fiber or fabric sinks in a basin of warm water, it is completely waterlogged and you know it is ready for the mordant or dyebath. For specific instructions on how to soak various materials, see appropriate sections on the pages that follow.

When Should I Mordant

There are three different points in the dye process at which fibers can be mordanted — before the dyebath (premordanting), during the dyebath (simultaneous mordanting), and after the dyebath (postmordanting). There are advantages and disadvantages to each method.

Premordanting

I prefer to premordant all wools in alum and cream of tartar before I dye them. I then overmordant with other chemicals, if a change of color is desired. It may be a little more work, but I like having the yarns mordanted and ready in case an opportunity comes along to try out a fresh new plant or delicate flower heads that I've just gathered or that a gardening friend gives me. This method also allows me to experiment by adding various skeins of yarn, each mordanted with different mordants, to the same dyebath and get a different color on each skein. If you use an iron-mordanted skein, make sure it is well rinsed before it is added it to the dyebath, or it will sadden the colors of all the other fibers. Although I use all three methods from time to time, depending on the effect I want, the premordanting method is the one that I use most often and the one I emphasize in this book. For complete directions on how to premordant, see pages 45–47.

Always remove the fiber from the dyebath before making any additions of water, assistants, or mordants.

Dyebath mordanting

Although the second method, dyebath mordanting, is a one-step method, and thus easier and faster, it has one main disadvantage — you cannot try out different mordants in the same dyebath. On the other hand, this method lends itself well to workshop situations, when time is of the essence and fast results are desired.

To mordant and dye fiber simultaneously, first prepare the dyebath, because you will leave the plant material in the pot while dyeing the fiber. Enclose the plant material in a stocking, gauze, or cheesecloth bag, otherwise you will have to pick or shake it from the fiber after dyeing. Add the mordant and some cream of tartar to the warm dyebath, and stir until dissolved. Add the wetted fiber and simmer for 1 hour. (If you add mordant or dye, always remove yarns or fibers from the pot first.) Let the yarns cool in the dyebath, or remove them and rinse in the same temperature water until the rinse water runs clear. Gently squeeze the excess water from the fiber, and hang it to dry.

An advantage of this method is that the more delicate plant materials (such as flower petals) and their resulting dyes do not simmer too long, and so the color remains clear.

Postmordanting

To brighten or darken the colors that you have already dyed, you may wish to mordant after the fiber is dyed. This is commonly called blooming or saddening. Tin and iron, respectively, are traditionally used for these effects.

To bloom or brighten fibers. During the last 15 to 20 minutes of dyeing, in 1 cup of warm water, dissolve ½ ounce of tin; in another cup of warm water, dissolve ½ ounce of cream of tartar. Remove the yarn from the dyebath, and turn off the heat. Quickly add the tin and cream of tartar solutions to the dyebath, and stir thoroughly. Put the fiber back into the dyebath and simmer an additional 15 minutes. Let the fiber cool in the pot, and then rinse with a little soap and let dry.

To sadden or dull fibers. During the last 15 to 20 minutes of dyeing, in 1 cup of warm water, dissolve ½ ounce of iron; in another cup of warm water, dissolve ½ ounce of cream of tartar. Remove the yarn from the dyebath, and turn off the heat. Add the iron and cream of

tartar solutions to the dyebath, and stir thoroughly. Put the fiber back into the dyebath, and simmer an additional 10 to 15 minutes. Let the fiber cool in the pot, and then rinse with a little soap and let dry.

Some dyers prefer to add the tin or iron solutions halfway through the dyeing process. However, prolonged exposure to either of these mordants can make fibers brittle or hard. Although the cream of tartar helps a little in this respect, I still prefer to add these two mordants at the end of the dyebath to reduce the fibers' exposure to them.

If you want to save the dyebaths for further use with other mordants, an alternate procedure for this method is to make up a separate mordant bath of tin (for blooming) or iron for saddening.

How Much Mordant To Use

The following formulas are the same whether you are premordanting, post-

Mordant Disposal

It is important to dispose of leftover mordant solutions properly. I try to use the least amount of mordant possible for the amount of material I am dyeing so that all of the mordant in the dyepot is absorbed into the fibers.

Some cities have "waste disposal days," when citizens can bring in chemicals, old paints, and so on. Alternatively, leftover dyebaths and mordant baths should be poured into an area away from water supplies, food gardens, or areas where pets eat or drink.

For more information on the proper use of mordants, see the article "Mordant Safety" by Rita Buchanan in *Dyes from Nature*.

mordanting, or mordanting simultaneously with the dyeing.

Alum. Use the following amount of alum (yarn is dry weight):

4 tablespoons alum per 1 pound yarn

or

1 tablespoon alum per 4 ounces yarn

or

¾ teaspoon alum per 1 ounce yarn

In addition, I add 1 ounce of cream of tartar to the alum bath for every 3 to 4 ounces of alum. Some dyers don't use cream of tartar at all, but I have found that it makes the yarn feel softer, as well as brightens the color.

Chrome. Use 3 teaspoons of chrome and 1 ounce of cream of tartar for every pound of wool dyed. For smaller amounts of wool, use proportionately less chrome. The chrome mordant bath should be kept covered at all times, as chrome is very light sensitive. It can also emit toxic fumes if not covered.

After the mordant bath has cooled, take off the cover and remove the wool. Rinse in warm water to wash out any excess chrome.

The wool should be used immediately, if possible. If not, store it in a black plastic bag in a dark place for up to two days. It is also acceptable, but less effective, to dry the wool away from light and store it in a brown paper bag for up to one week in a dark closet or drawer.

Tannin. Use 1 ounce of tannin per pound of wool.

Tin. Use ½ ounce of tin or less per pound of wool, in addition to ½ ounce of cream of tartar. Rinse in soapy water before dyeing.

Iron. Use 2 tablespoons of iron per pound of wool. Gently stir the yarn occasionally to prevent streaking.

Tips for Handling Wools

◆ Do not change the temperature of wools suddenly.
◆ Do not boil wool — this causes shrinkage.
◆ Move wool back and forth *gently* while mordanting or dyeing. Too much stirring or agitation causes matting, shrinkage, or felting.
◆ Never wring or twist wool to remove moisture — gently *squeeze* it with your hands.
◆ Never hold saturated wool over the dyepot to drain — the fibers stretch and weaken when filled with water. Hold a large strainer or colander over the pot and place the wool in it to drain.

Copper. Use 2 tablespoons of copper per pound of wool with 1 ounce cream of tartar.

General Instructions for Premordanting

The following instructions apply to all mordants. Refer to the chart on pages 40–41 for advice on how much mordant to use.

Mordanting Wool Yarns

Put yarn into 1- or 4-ounce skeins. Many books on natural dyeing give directions and recipes for dyeing 1 pound of yarn, but because most of the projects in this book use only a small amount of any given color, I've scaled down the basic recipes. Working with small amounts makes better sense, too, when you are just beginning to experiment with natural dyes; you don't want to risk wasting a whole pound of yarn on a color that you might not like. When you become more experienced or if your project is a larger one, you will want to dye larger quantities of yarns.

You don't have to start out with expensive, brand-new yarns or fibers for your first dyeing experiments. For real economy, you can even unravel the yarn from an old moth-chewed white or beige sweater. Wash the yarn and rewind it into skeins before you dye it.

1. Fill a clean sink, pot, or basin with warm, soapy water (1 or 2 small drops of a mild dishwashing liquid, such as Ivory Liquid). Put the dry wool in and soak until well wetted. This relaxes the fibers, "fluffs them up," and helps them better absorb the mordants and dyes. If you are using raw wool, see page 35 for washing and scouring instructions.

The key to handling wools (whether raw fibers, yarn, or fabrics) is to be gentle — do not change temperature suddenly; do not agitate the fibers; do not wring or stretch them while wet. If you ignore these rules, you'll soon learn the hard way how to make felt — whether you want to or not!

2. Place enough warm water in a 4-gallon nonreactive (enamel or stainless steel) pot to cover the amount of wool that you're dyeing. The wool should have room to float in the water — it should not be crowded.

3. Mix the required amount (see pages 40–41) of mordant and assistant in a little hot water in a jar, and shake or stir until dissolved. Add this mixture to the water in the pot, and stir until well mixed.

4. Rinse the soap from the wool with warm water, and gently squeeze water out. Put the wool in the pot with the mordant solution.

5. Bring the water to a simmer (180° to 200°F), and simmer the wool in this solution for 1 hour *without* boiling. Occasionally turn the wool over gently in the pot. Make sure it remains totally immersed in the solution after you stir it. Boiling can cause the wool to shrink, so don't let the water get beyond a simmer. Fine wool yarns may require simmering for only 45 minutes, whereas heavier yarns should be simmered for at least an hour. Always allow at least 45 minutes so that the fiber can properly absorb the mordant. Add more water (of the same simmering temperature) through the process to keep it at the same level in the pot. For this purpose, I usually keep a teakettle simmering on the back burner on low heat. Always remove the wool before adding additional water.

6. Turn off the heat after 1 hour, and let the wool cool in the solution until lukewarm, or better yet, overnight. This will make the fibers easier to handle and allow them more time to bond with the mordant.

7. Remove the wool from the mordant bath, rinse in water that is the same temperature as the mordant bath and gently squeeze or place in a colander and allow to drain.

8. At this point, you can dye the wool immediately if you wish. To store it for further dyeing, dry in a dark place or in the shade outside, or store it in a plastic bag in the refrigerator for no longer than 3 weeks (check the bags daily for mold or mildew). If

Ageing the Mordant

There is some evidence that dyebaths produce better results if fibers are allowed to "age" for a while after the mordanting process. In her book *Weaving*, Shirley Held suggests that after the yarn has been removed from the mordant solution, it be wrapped in a bath towel and allowed to sit for at least 24 hours. (Chrome-mordanted yarns should be completely covered.) In my own experience, cotton fabrics also seem to dye better if they are allowed to "air" for a few days after mordanting and before dyeing.

you refrigerate the wool, let it come to room temperature before adding it to a dyebath.

Mordanting Wool Fabrics

Wool fabrics are mordanted in much the same way as yarns, using the same amounts of chemicals and assistants. When dyeing wool yardage for quilts or hooked rugs, I cut the fabric into smaller pieces (usually ¼ yard) so they will move around more freely in the dyebath. Fabrics need to be gently stirred and turned over in the dyepot more often than yarns, because they have a tendency to spot and dye unevenly if not moved. It is also better to strain all the dyestuff out of the bath before you dye wool fabrics; darker spots occur if the fabric comes in contact with dyestuffs like cochineal and logwood. (I have some lovely pink polka-dot fabric left from this experiment!)

Mordanting Cottons, Linens, and Other Plant Fibers

Different authorities recommend a number of ways to mordant cottons and linens. They are all similar, however, in that they involve a combination of alum and tannic acid for the mordanting solution.

Because of their unique properties, cottons and other cellulose (or plant) fibers do not bind to the metallic mordant salts as easily as those of wool. Plant fibers do bind readily with tannic acid, however, and it is thus sometimes used alone as a mordant or as an assistant. Jim Liles (*The Art and Craft of Natural Dyeing*) suggests that the tannic acid serves as a "bridge" linking the mordant to the fibers.

Mordanting cotton yarns or fabrics is very similar to mordanting wools, but because plant fibers are not as susceptible to high temperatures, they can be safely boiled while mordanting.

There are two main methods to mordant cottons: an easier method, and a more complicated, traditional procedure.

The easier method, which I use most often, is adapted from Karen Leigh Casselman's book *Craft of the Dyer: Colour from Plants and Lichens of the Northeast*. I used this method for most of the cotton fabrics in the quilt shown on page 124. It is for 1 pound of fabric; change the amounts proportionately if you want to dye more or less fabric.

1. Soak fiber or fabric in warm water for several hours or until well wetted. Some fabrics ready for dyeing (such as those available from Testfabrics; see address in Appendix) do not need to soak for this long. If you are

---

Mordanting Cotton Embroidery Floss

Several small skeins of cotton embroidery floss can be mordanted at the same time with the fabric . These should be opened out, made into small looped skeins and tied securely at each end and several places in between, and put into a knee-high hose, so they don't become entangled with the fabric. This is an important step: I've found cotton embroidery floss tangles worse than any other yarn or fiber that I've ever dyed! The mordant penetrates into the hose and mordants the floss simultaneously with the fabric.

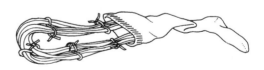

The fabric and the floss come out of the mordant bath with a slightly tannish tint to them. This is normal: it's the tannin that causes it.

using 100 percent cotton fabrics purchased from a fabric store, you need to wash them well in hot, soapy water first before mordanting. These fabrics probably have been treated with chemicals or have picked up soil or oils from handling, which can block dye absorption.

2. Dissolve 3 tablespoons alum in a small amount of boiling water. Add this to 2 gallons of water and stir well.
3. Dissolve 1 tablespoon of tannic acid in a small amount of boiling water and add to bath.
4. Add more water until pot is two-thirds full *before* you add the fabric.
5. Add the wet fabric, and increase the heat until the water comes to a boil. Stir the fabric down so that all surfaces come in contact with the water. Boil for 15 more minutes, then remove pot from heat.
6. Leave the fabric to cool in the solution overnight. This is essential. In fact, the longer you can leave the fabric in the solution, the better.
7. Rinse the mordanted fabric, and hang it in the shade to dry. If dyeing is to take place in the near future, the fabric can be stored damp in a plastic bag until needed. Refrigerate it for up to a week. Cotton fabrics seem to take dye better if allowed to hang and dry for a few days before dyeing.

A second (and more complicated) procedure for mordanting plant fibers such as cotton or linen is described by both Rita Buchanan in her book *A Weaver's Garden* and by Jim Liles in his *The Art and Craft of Natural Dyeing,* as well as by a number of other authors. It is a two-step process and takes slightly longer than the shorter method outlined above. It is said to make the fabrics more lightfast, but I've found no noticeable difference between cotton fabrics mordanted in this matter and those mordanted by the easier method. It does seem to make

some linen fabrics take dye better.

Begin by following steps 1 through 6 above, and then proceed as follows:

7. Rinse the mordanted fabric.
8. Prepare a second mordant bath and repeat steps 2 to 6 above.

Mordanting Silks

Silks, like wools and other animal fibers, easily combine with mordants. The procedure for mordanting silk (both fabrics and yarns) is a bit different from that for wool, however. In her book *Natural Dyes,* Sallie Pease Kierstead recommends dissolving the mordant and adding it to enough water to cover the silk completely. After thoroughly wetting the silk, put it in the mordant solution and bring the temperature to about 100°F. Turn off the heat and allow the fabric to sit in the solution from 12 to 15 hours, or overnight. Kierstead also recommends dyeing the silk immediately after this setting time, before it dries.

Silk should never be mordanted with iron.

Other experts recommend using the same mordanting method for silk as for wool, with one difference: Keep the temperature at 160°F and do not simmer the fiber. This seems to preserve the lustrous quality of the silk. It is the method that I most often use for silk fabrics.

Mordanting Basketry Fibers

The method that I use to mordant basketry fibers, such as basketry splint, cane, raffia, and cornhusks, is very similar to the short method for mordanting other plant fibers, such as cottons or linens, described above. I have had good results dyeing cornhusks that were mordanted only with alum and cream of tartar.

To prepare materials for mordanting, coil them into small bundles for easier handling, and soak them in very hot water until they have absorbed the maximum amount of water possible. When they sink under water, they are thoroughly saturated.

Prepare a mordant bath with alum and tannin (see pages 40–41). Place the basketry materials in the pot and boil for at least 1 hour. I leave them in the pot to cool overnight (or as long as possible), so that they can continue to soak up the mordants.

Remove the materials from the pot and allow them to drain on a pile of old newspapers. Because the materials must be re-wetted if they dry completely before dyeing, it is most convenient to dye them while they are still wet from mordanting. It is also better for the fibers, as they have a tendency to break down if subjected to too much water and heat.

 **chapter 4**

Dyeing
Natural Fibers

three classifications of natural dyes indicate how natural fibers react with them: Direct (or substantive) dyes, adjective (or mordant) dyes, and vat dyes. In this book, I have tried to include a good representation of all three types of dyes.

Direct dyes are easily soluble in water and require no mordants. Some of the materials that yield direct dyes include annatto, barberry, black walnut hulls, dock, lichens, oak bark and galls, safflower, staghorn moss, and turmeric.

In contrast, *adjective dyes* require the addition of mordants to bind to the fibers and to be permanent. Most natural dyes belong to this group.

Vat dyes, which include indigo and woad, are the rarest dyes occurring in nature. These dyes are insoluble in water and must react with chemicals or bacterias that change them from insoluble to soluble before they can be used to color fibers.

Making the Dyebath

Making the dyebath is perhaps the most rewarding step of the natural dyeing process. Basically, a dyebath is water in which plant material has been boiled and simmered for whatever length of time it takes to release the colors.

The amount of dye material that should be used in relation to a certain amount of water is not a hard-and-fast rule. A good, basic ratio of plant material to fibers, however, can be used as a starting point. Simply stated, use twice as much plant material as fibers:

2 parts plant material   *1 part water*   *1 part fiber*

A Note About Color Names

Every person who works with color has her or his own idea of what a particular color looks like. For instance, if I say that a yarn is yellowish green, 500 different people may have 500 (or more) different ideas about the color. The colors noted on the Basic Dyeplant Chart beginning on page 5 give you a basic idea of the color range (and possibilities) inherent in a certain dyestuff. You will (most likely) produce a color — call it what you will — within the same range.

Of course, the more plant material that you use, the darker the dyebath will be. If you have less dyestuff, remember that the color will not be as dark as if you had used more; or, just use less yarn.

The *ratio* of *plant material* to fiber is more critical than the *amount of water* used. The basic function of the water is simply to dissolve the dye and distribute it evenly throughout the pot. A good rule of thumb is to use at least 1 quart of water to every ounce of yarn or fiber you are dyeing, but it doesn't really matter how much water you have in your dyepot to start with, as long as you have enough in the pot so that the fiber can "swim" freely without being bunched up. You can keep adding water during the dyeing process without diluting the strength of the colors.

Dyeing with Herbs and Flowers

Generally speaking, fresh, dried, or frozen flowers or herbs can be added to the dyebath. When using dried flower heads, use a bit less than if using fresh ones. The exceptions are dandelion and goldenrod flowers, both of which should be used only while fresh.

Gather the flower heads or the herb leaves when they are at their peak, cover with cold water, and boil for approximately 1 hour or until the petals look drained or bleached of all color. Strain the liquid into a pot, and add enough water to make a 4-gallon solution (for 1 pound or less of fiber). Immerse the wet, mordanted fibers in the bath, heat almost to boiling, and simmer for 1 hour. Allow the dyebath to cool slightly, remove the fiber, rinse in the same temperature of water, and dry. This method can be used with marigolds, zinnias, coreopsis, cosmos, onion skins, and tender leaves of herbs such as mint or sage.

Dyeing with Leaves

Gather leaves and chop or cut them into small pieces. You can use a leaf chopper/shredder, if you have one and want to use a large amount of plant material. Follow the general guidelines as mentioned above for flowers, but boil the leaves for 1 hour or longer to release the dye matter.

Dyeing with Berries

Gather berries as soon as possible after they ripen. It takes a lot of berries to get a good, rich, strong dyebath, so gather a gallon for every 2 to 4 ounces of wool. Mash all of the juice out of the berries, strain out the remaining berry particles, and use the juice in a simmering (not boiling) dyebath.

Dyeing with Roots and Barks

Barks, twigs, roots, and other woody materials release their color more slowly than the more dainty flower petals and leaves. Chop, shred, or grind them into small pieces (about 1 to 3 inches long) to release more of their coloring matter. I have used several different tools for doing this — including a hammer on a concrete driveway! The most successful method was an old meat grinder. Soak the prepared materials from 12 to 24 hours. Bring the water and materials to a boil, and simmer vigorously for 5 or 6 hours (except for madder, which should *not* be boiled), making sure to keep adding water as it evaporates. The boiling time varies with the materials being used, of course, but in most cases it takes this long for the coloring matter in woody material to be fully released. Keep boiling until the material releases no more color.

Dyeing the Fibers

The techniques for dyeing fleece, yarn, fabric, and other materials vary only slightly. Here are some tips.

Dyeing Raw Fleece

You can put small amounts of clean fleece destined for spinning or felting projects into a nylon hose, and add it to your regular dyebath along with yarns. When you are dyeing a whole fleece, handle the wool as little as possible. Use the simultaneous method of dyeing, prepare a dyebath with the required plant materials and the mordants (see pages 40–41). Let the dyebath cool and strain out the plant materials before adding the wetted, warm wool. Proceed with dyeing just as for yarns.

Dyeing Wool Yarn

Make the yarn into skeins of desired weight. If you are dyeing a smaller (or larger) amount of wool than you usually dye, adjust the amounts of mordants, water, and dyestuffs proportionately. Small skeins absorb the dye faster and more uniformly; sometimes it takes large skeins an incredibly long time to dry. If you make small ones, you can speed up the process a bit.

Be sure to tie the skeins with white string; colored string may "bleed" into your dyebath or onto your yarns and change the color.

Dyeing Cotton Fabric

In general, fabrics are more difficult to dye evenly than are yarns. It is important that these steps be followed to produce a uniform color throughout the fabric.

When dyeing cotton fabrics, use more water in the dyepot than you would normally use for wool yarns. The fiber should have plenty of room to move around in the dyebath. It is important to work the fabric around in the dyebath periodically. Be sure that the fabric doesn't sit on the bottom of the pot for long periods of time as this will cause splotching and uneven dyeing.

Simmer the fabric in the dyebath for at least 1 hour; let it cool in the dyebath. Remove from the dyebath, wash with gentle soap, and then rinse well. Hang to dry.

Dyeing Cotton Embroidery Threads

Thoroughly wet premordanted cotton embroidery flosses and put them into your dyepot along with your wools. Unless you are dyeing more than two or three of these small skeins, they add little bulk to the dyepot.

Dyeing Silk

The process of dyeing silk is similar to the one used for wool, with a few exceptions. Since silk has slightly less affinity for plant dyes, you need more dye material to make a stronger dyebath. In addition, keep the temperature of the dyebath a little lower than that for wool (about 185°F) to preserve the lustrous quality of the silk. To get the deepest colors possible, let the silk stay in the dyebath a bit longer, even overnight if necessary. Rinse the yarn or fabric thoroughly, and hang to dry.

Although all dyes can be used on silks, those that have proven especially successful include cochineal, indigo, madder, turmeric, weld, pokeberry, logwood, and marigold.

Dyeing Basketry Materials

I've successfully dyed basketry materials such as sisal, cornhusks, raffia, and wooden splint with natural dyes. Mordant with the simpler of the cotton/linen methods. It is better to dye these materials immediately after mordanting, when they are already thoroughly wetted. Better still, follow simultaneous mordanting/dyeing procedures, because many basketry materials are more fragile and do not hold up well when heated or soaked for long periods of time.

Basketmaker Jim Bennett of Deer Track Crafts in Chelsea, Michigan, uses a few strands of naturally dyed colors in his beautiful split oak and ash baskets. He dyes these woods with bloodroot, black walnut hulls, osage orange, and sassafrass, and does not use mordants.

Susanna Reppert of The Rosemary House in Mechanicsburg, Pennsylvania, has produced a nice, dark tan from sassafras on the splint and a medium rosy pink with cochineal on splint for weaving chair seats.

Try to keep natural fiber basketry materials submerged in the dyebath. They tend to float at times and should be pushed down into the water as much as possible. The materials sink as they absorb water from the dyepot. Basketry splint and reed are easier to handle if they are coiled into small bundles. If you are dyeing materials specifically for a project, you can cut the individual pieces before mordanting or dyeing to make them easier to handle.

Bring the dyebath to a boil (unless using madder) and simmer 1 hour. Periodically turn the materials over in the pot so that they can absorb the color evenly on all sides. Let the materials cool in the dyebath overnight, if possible.

SOME DYE RESULTS ON CORNHUSKS

DYE	RESULT
Annatto (exhaust bath) (no mordant)	Light orange
Coffee (no mordant)	Tan
Indigo	Medium green
Logwood	Dark purple
Logwood (no mordant)	Grayish purple
Madder (exhaust bath)	Coral
Marigold/coreopsis (no mordant)	Medium yellow
Onion skins	Medium yellow
Osage orange	Yellow
Purple basil (no mordant)	Medium pink
Turmeric (no mordant)	Bright yellow
Turmeric	Medium yellow

(Cornhusks were mordanted with alum and cream of tartar before dyeing unless otherwise indicated.)

SOME DYE RESULTS ON BASKETRY SPLINT

DYE	RESULT
Cochineal	Dark pink
Indigo	Dark blue
Indigo (1-minute dip)	Light blue
Madder	Melon red
Marigold/coreopsis	Medium yellow
Osage orange	Light yellow
Sassafras	Dark tan
Sumac	Tan
Turmeric	Bright yellow
Turmeric + indigo	Emerald green
Turmeric + indigo	Lime green (1-minute dip)

Remove materials from the pot and drain on a stack of old newspapers until needed. Many basketry projects require that the materials be damp when you work with them, so it might be a good idea to schedule the dyeing session right before you intend to use the splint or reed. This keeps you from having to rewet the fibers an additional time.

I obtained some beautiful, surprising colors on basketry splint using indigo, cochineal, madder, turmeric, sumac, and osage orange, including a bright green using turmeric with an indigo overdye.

When you dye cornhusks or other basketry materials, their natural colors contribute to their final colors. For instance, when I dyed cornhusks with indigo, the result was a green instead of the deep blue that I had expected. I couldn't get a full range of colors on the yellowish cornhusks.

Some Alternative Dyeing Methods

Sometimes it's fun to try methods other than the traditional dye-vat-over-heat. Here are a few I've enjoyed experimenting with.

Solar Dyeing

Solar dyeing techniques deserve more attention. On the several occasions I experimented in this area, I was quite pleased with the outcome. For example, I premordanted several small skeins of yarn (1 ounce each) with alum, and dyed them with a mixture of marigold and coreopsis flowers to get a bright golden color. After solar postmordanting with copper, the yarns turned an attractive light olive green. Here's the procedure that I followed:

1. Fill a quart jar with hot water. Stir in 1 teaspoon copper and stir well until dissolved. (Remember, always add chemical to water — not water to chemicals!)
2. Add well-wetted dyed yarns. Fasten on the lid, and put the jar outside in the sun.
3. Stir the yarn in the jar occasionally, until the desired color is reached. Remember that some of the color will rinse out, and the yarn will dry a shade or two lighter.
4. Remove the yarn, rinse, and dry.

·The jar sat on my aggregate patio during the summer when temperatures outside reached over 100°F. The sun, combined with the heat reflected from the patio surface, pushed the temperature of the water in the glass jar to between 115° and 120°F; temperatures at night were about 75°F. Keeping the mordant at these temperatures for three or four days seemed sufficient to cause the mordant and the dyes to act on the yarns and change their color. Temperatures don't get this hot in all climates, of course, but you may enjoy your own experimentation, perhaps with home-built solar ovens or reflectors.

In addition to dyeing small skeins of yarn, I solar-dyed some washed, mordanted wool fleece with brazilwood, with equal success. Here is my method for dyeing the fleece:

1. Put 1 tablespoon of brazilwood in the bottom of a gallon glass jar.
2. Pour in 1 cup of boiling water. Stir.
3. Fill jar three quarters full with warm water.
4. Wet wool with warm water, and add to jar.
5. Put lid on jar, and set it in strong sunlight.
6. Check daily for color and take out when desired color is reached. (Allow for the fact that the color will be approximately one shade lighter when the wool is dry.)
7. Rinse wool and dry.

Rita Buchanan (*A Weaver's Garden*) suggests using safflower as a solar dye (see method for dyeing with safflower on pages 78–79). Instead of using the red dye pigment in a traditional dyebath, place it in a glass jar, along with the fibers to be dyed, and set it in the sun for several hours.

Other dye materials that may be tried with the solar dyeing method are walnut hulls and bark, goldenrod flowers, and marigold petals, as well as cactus fruit, madder, logwood, and turmeric. For the cactus fruit, use the *steeping, or fermentation, method* of dyeing. Also called *putrefaction dyeing* (for obvious reasons), in this method dyeplants are layered together with the fiber and left to ferment for several days or several weeks. Sometimes urine was used in the dyebath instead of water. The Navajos have used this method with prickly pear cactus fruits to make beautiful pinks and reds on tapestry wools.

Overdyeing

We have covered the basics of fiber preparation, mordanting, and natural dyeing using single-dye materials. A whole new range of colors can be produced by overdyeing (or topdyeing) one color with another to produce a third and different color. Traditionally, this method has been used to produce the color known as *Saxon green* by overdyeing yarn that has been dyed yellow using weld with the blue from woad.

The simplest form of overdyeing is to dye naturally colored wools to get a host of different colors and effects. For instance, natural wool yarns and fleeces can be white, gray, mixed, and even black. By dyeing over these colors with natural dyes, you can obtain heathered effects. I enjoy using these in tapestries when I want colors with a gray cast to blend with other yarns. I feel that the heathered yarns give more depth to the piece, making it more interesting.

Overdyeing also works well on old yarns that are not quite the right color — or are a bit outdated colorwise. I've mordanted and overdyed high-quality beige needlepoint yarns (100 percent wool), purchased at garage sales and second-hand stores, and transformed them into beautiful shades. You can also overdye your own home-dyed yarns when the first color is not really what you expected or wanted — or if it is just plain ugly!

Some of the literature suggests that yarns can be both mordanted and topmordanted — mordanted once again after the first dyebath, before the second dyebath. If you use different mordants, you can achieve new colors — a starting point for some more interesting experiments.

Although it is a gamble, yarns can sometimes be overdyed in order to match. While working on the needlepoint pillow in the project section, I ran out of the greenish blue color. For the original color, I had used turmeric, plus an indigo overdye. I tried overdyeing a skein of turmeric-dyed yarn with indigo. The result was a beautiful emerald green color — exciting, but did not even closely match. When I tried the reverse — dyeing indigo-dyed yarn with turmeric — I got a match, after an additional dip in the indigo vat.

From this I learned three lessons:

◆ Overdyeing can produce some beautiful colors (such as the emerald green) that are impossible to achieve with single dyestuffs.

◆ Always dye enough yarn for a project before starting it!

◆ Don't ever assume *anything* in natural dyeing. This is perhaps a frustrating lesson, but after all, this is one of the reasons I like natural dyeing. You can work around the few limitations in the art, as long as you follow a few simple rules.

The following basic color combinations

SOME POSSIBILITIES FOR OVERDYEING

DYE 1	DYE 2	RESULTING COLOR	MORDANT	FIBERS
Turmeric	Cochineal	Orange	Tin	Wool
Fustic	Madder	Orange	Alum + tin	All
Cutch	Madder	Rust, red-browns	Alum	Wool
Madder	Yellow onion skins	Orange	Alum	Wool
Madder	Yellow onion skins	Light orange	Alum	Other fibers
Pokeberries	Red onion skins	Rust	Alum	Wool, silk, linen, cotton
Annatto	Red onion skins	Dark yellow (bright)	Tin	Wool, silk
Fustic	Indigo	Various greens*	Alum	Wool, silk
Indigo	Turmeric	Bright greens	Alum	Wool, silk
Turmeric	Indigo	Teal green*	Alum	Wool
Turmeric	Indigo	Clear green*	Alum	Cornhusks
Turmeric	Indigo	Dark emerald green*	Alum	Basketry splint
Barberry	Indigo	Bright green*	None	Wool
Madder	Indigo	Purple*	Alum	Wool
Madder	Indigo	Navy blue*	Chrome + iron	Wool
Cochineal	Indigo	Purple; lavender*	Alum	Wool, silk
Cochineal	Indigo	Lighter shades	Alum	Cotton
Cochineal	Madder	Brownish purple	Alum	Wool, silk
Cochineal	Madder	Lighter shades	Alum	Linen, cotton
Madder	Mullein	Brownish red	Alum	Wool, silk, linen, cotton
Black walnut hulls	Indigo	Black*	Alum	Wool, silk
Black walnut hulls	Indigo	Shades of gray	Alum	Linen, cotton

*Note: Repeated dippings into the indigo vat deepens the subsequent color.

may come in helpful for overdyeing:

Yellow + red = orange
Yellow + blue = green
Blue + green = turquoise or teal
Blue + red = purple
Blue + brown = dull, dark brown

The clarity of the colors you achieve with overdyeing depends on the quality of the color you start with. For example, if you overdye a muddy yellow-gold with blue you will probably get a muddy olive-green rather than a clear, bright emerald green. To get clear, true green, use a clear yellow instead (from weld or turmeric, for example), and overdye with indigo.

To achieve greater control, begin with weak, light colors and overdye them with dark colors.

Overdyed yarns can be used effectively where gradations of a single color are needed. If you have yarns or fibers that have previously been dyed in less-than-exciting colors, put them all together into the same dyebath of a second color. The resulting colors, although different, will be harmonious and can be used together in a project.

In the chart on page 56 I show some possibilities for overdyeing. In most cases, the fibers were dyed with the first material, rinsed, allowed to drain or dry, and overdyed with the second material. Although you could actually mix the dye materials in the same dyebath, I have not found this to be as effective as using two separate dyebaths. Remember to thoroughly re-wet the fiber before the second dyebath if it has been allowed to dry between dyebaths.

Cross-Dyeing

Yarns that contain two or more different fibers sometimes take dye in interesting ways. Because the different fibers take dyes differently, you may get a yarn of two different

colors or two different shades of the same color. Some fibers even resist dye completely, and your dyed yarn will be heathered, with flecks of white all through it.

Afterbaths

Routinely, most fibers should be rinsed after dyeing and before drying. At this stage, it is sometimes possible to make a dramatic last-minute change in color by adding an alkaline or acid substance to the last rinse water. You can use white vinegar (acetic acid) or even lemon juice as acid rinses, or clear, nonsudsing ammonia or common baking soda as alkaline rinses. These rinses cause chemical reactions that shift the pH balance of the yarns, resulting in a change of color. Not all dyestuffs respond to these rinses, but some, such as brazilwood and logwood, change dramatically. For instance, a wool yarn mordanted with alum and dyed with logwood results in a pretty medium lavender color; rinsed in baking soda and water, however, the color changes to a beautiful dark blue-violet. Brazilwood on wool yarn with an alum mordant produces a deep coral color; rinsed in baking soda and water, the color changes to a bright magenta. Yellows are intensified when rinsed with ammonia; oranges (such as from coreopsis) tend to turn redder when rinsed with ammonia; blues and purples are brightened and turned redder when rinsed with vinegar; and alkaline rinses sometimes give a greenish tint to blue colors. Try various rinses for yourself — they're like magic!

Microwave Dyeing

Microwave ovens can serve as a heat source for dyeing small amounts of naturally dyed yarns and fibers. Use only food-safe dyes and only alum as a mordant, unless you have a microwave that you can use exclusively for dye projects. Dye residue may collect on the oven surfaces and subsequently contaminate food.

LIGHTFASTNESS OF VARIOUS DYES

This chart notes the degrees of lightfastness that you can expect from dyes from various plants. It was compiled from my own tests and notes on lightfastness, as well as from other printed sources (see Suggested Reading, page 150).

Agrimony	Very good		Dock	Very good
Alder	Excellent		Hops	Good
Ash	Excellent		Indigo	Good to excellent
Aspen	Excellent		Madder	Good to excellent
Aster	Good to excellent (depending on species)		Marigold	Excellent
			Mint	Very good
Barberry	Excellent		Mullein	Good
Bayberry	Excellent		Onion	Very good
Bedstraw, lady's	Good		Pokeberry	Good
Beech	Good for bark; excellent for leaves		Safflower	Good
			Sage	Good
Black walnut	Excellent		Sumac	Very good
Burdock	Good		Sunflower	Very good
Cabbage, purple	Bad to good (depending on fiber)		Tansy	Fair to good
			Toadflax	Good
Cochineal	Excellent		Tomato	fair to good
Coneflower	Excellent		Turmeric	good
Coreopsis	Excellent		Weld	excellent
Cosmos	Excellent		Woad	excellent
Dandelion	Good to very good		Yarrow	excellent

To dye in a microwave oven use a strong dyebath in a covered Pyrex, Visions by Corning, or other microwave-proof bowl. "Cook" the dyebath and fiber together in the bowl for several minutes, or until the fiber absorbs the coloring matter — the length of time depends on the wattage of your microwave.

Fibers dyed by this method seem adequately lightfast, and because the raw fibers aren't agitated, no felting or matting occurs.

Dyeing with Children

Children are fascinated to learn that you can get colors from plants. It is a magical process that they seem never to tire of seeing. You can share this magic with them by showing them some of the possibilities of natural dyes. Naturally Dyed Easter Eggs (pages 143–144) and the Cornhusk Wreath and Angel (pages 137–142) are projects that they may particularly enjoy.

Some safe dyes to use with children include acorns, onion skins, tea, coffee, henna, turmeric, black walnut hulls, annatto, and logwood. Some of these need only alum with cream of tartar as mordants; some need no mordant at all. (In one experiment, yarn that I dyed with annatto was actually twice as bright on an unmordanted sample as on the mordanted wool.) Many of the grocery store dyes mentioned in chapter 7 are also safe and suitable for children's dyeing projects.

Testing for Fastness

Testing natural dyes for fastness to light and washing is an important step in the process. Some plants are fast with one mordant on wool, but not as fast on cotton. Some colors change and mellow when exposed to sunlight, although they do not change color completely. Depending on how the fibers will be used, colorfastness is more or less of a concern. For example, you may not care that a hooked rug is not washfast, as you'll probably dry clean or spot clean it. If you are making clothing, however, you want the colors to be both washfast and lightfast.

Although there are many ways to test dyes for lightfastness, the easiest way is to hang several lengths of yarn halfway in and halfway out of a closed box on a bright, sunny windowsill. Or, tape or hang pieces of dyed fabrics in a sunny window for a period of time and compare them with pieces of the same fabric that have been stored in a dark place. To test washfastness, place a small length of yarn or piece of fabric in a jar with mild soap and warm water. Shake the jar and notice what happens. Does the color bleed into the water? Or, place the wet yarn on a white cloth and notice whether the color bleeds onto it.

Factors That Affect Colors

There are many variables and changing factors that can affect the color given by dye plants. Just a few of these are the climate; whether the season has been especially hot, sunny, and dry, or cold and wet; the time of day (or year) when the plant is gathered; the soil content of the plant's home; the general health of the plant; and the softness or hardness (the pH reading) of the water used in the dyebath.

Just as soil, weather, and season influence the quality of a flower's bloom or a vegetable harvest, they also influence the colors created from plants. Plants are products of their environments, so it is not hard to see why two identical plants from the same garden on the same day could make two completely different colors.

WHAT WENT WRONG?

PROBLEM	REASON	SOLUTION
Wool feels sticky	Too much alum	Try rinsing in cream of tartar before dyeing; use less alum next time.
Color on fabrics is splotchy or spotty	Not enough water or room in dyepot; not stirred often enough	Use in projects such as quilts, or sewn or hooked rugs; try again.
Wool is brittle; harsh to touch	Too much tin	Use soap in rinse water; try again; use yarn in non-clothing project.
Streaked yarns or fabrics	Chrome mordant bath was exposed to light	Try to "level" color with Glauber's salt or overdye with darker color.
Crocking (the color rubs off on one's hands)	Improper rinsing of the dyed fiber	Re-wet fiber and rinse; add a few drops of neutral soap, if needed.

Some exciting new research by Martha Weiss of the University of California at Berkeley, reported in the *Austin American-Statesman* (November 1991), suggests that many flowering plants attract their insect pollinators and direct them to their fertile blossoms by changing the colors of individual flowers from one day to the next. The plants do this, Weiss states, by activating the production of a deep crimson pigment called *anthocyanin*. After the flower is pollinated by the insect, the levels of the pigment fall back down to the previous levels. For plants containing anthocyanin, perhaps this explains why you can get two different colors from the same group of flowers on two separate days.

Water Used for Dyeing

The water that you use in your dyebath affects the color of your dyed fibers. Ideally, soft water with little mineral content is best for dyeing, scouring, and even rinsing yarn; however, this is often hard to obtain. Tap water contains minerals, chemicals, contaminants, and other surprises. Even rainwater is not safe in many areas, as world pollution levels rise.

You can check your own water for hardness or softness and mineral content by using litmus papers or other indicator papers that can be purchased from a drugstore or a pet shop. This simple test will tell you if your water is more alkaline or acid than normal and give you some idea of the color ranges that you can expect from using this water.

You can change the pH balance of your water by adding 1 teaspoon of borax or 2 tablespoons of vinegar per gallon of water in your dyepot.

Although the water in my community is very heavy with limestone deposits, I haven't found that it adversely affects my dyebaths. The best plan, I think, is just to accept the color differences that your water creates.

Exhaust Baths

Many dyebaths can be used over and over again as long as they contain color. After you have achieved the results you want for the main part of your dye project, make use of any residual dye by adding small amounts of clean, premordanted fleece or small skeins of yarn. These *exhaust baths* use up the remaining color in the dyepot, and you will often get lovely pastel shades of your first color. If you are a spinner, you can combine several of these colors to make a unique, handspun rainbow yarns. Or, use these small bits of colored fleece for felting projects or as texture in a tapestry. Use the small skeins of wool for needlepoint or crewel projects.

You can also use exhaust baths to experiment with new combinations or mordants, and thus be more adventurous than you might with a fresh dyepot of a limited plant or flower.

Preserving Dyebaths

You can preserve a dyebath for use several months later by adding 1 teaspoon of sodium benzoate per gallon of liquid. Store the bath in an airtight container. Purchase or order sodium benzoate from chemical suppliers or a large pharmacy or drugstore.

Depending on your climate and the plant used, some dyebaths can be stored in tightly capped glass jars for some time even without added sodium benzoate as a preservative.

You can preserve unmordanted dyebaths almost forever with little color change by freezing them. Fill sturdy plastic or glass containers (no metal containers) no more than three quarters full, and place them in the freezer with the cover off until frozen. *Make sure they're well labelled!* Simply thaw and they're ready for use.

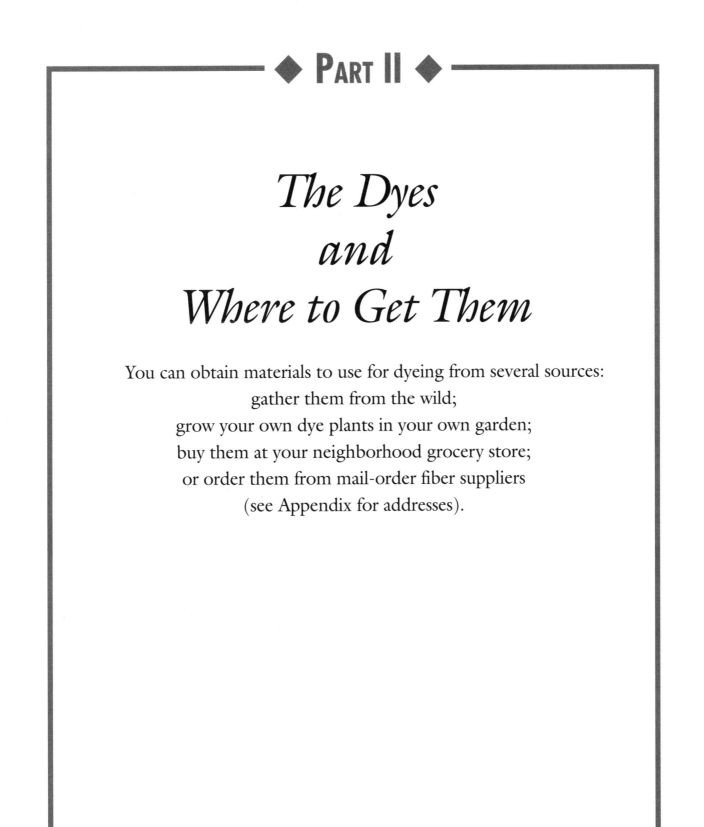

◆ PART II ◆

The Dyes
and
Where to Get Them

You can obtain materials to use for dyeing from several sources:
gather them from the wild;
grow your own dye plants in your own garden;
buy them at your neighborhood grocery store;
or order them from mail-order fiber suppliers
(see Appendix for addresses).

☕ chapter 5 ☕

Dyes to Gather

*J*ust as there is a best time of year for planting certain plants, there is also a best time of year for harvesting dye materials. Berries and fruits like poke-berry, grapes, sumac, and blackberries, should be picked when they are ripe. Nuts should be collected as soon as they fall to the ground. Roots are best when gathered in the fall. Barks and tree roots are best when gathered between February and June, when they'll produce the most intense color. Remember that removing a large quantity of bark from a living tree will most likely kill the tree. Gather bark from the ground, from firewood, or from prunings of tree limbs.

Hot, dry weather generally produces plants that give off intense colors.

Collect dye plants, twigs, and leaves in a large, porous paper bag, which allows the materials to "breathe." Do not gather or store dye plants in plastic bags unless you will be using them immediately; moisture collects in the airless environment and quickly causes mold and mildew — and ruined dye materials.

With some exceptions, there are strong seasonal trends in the particular colors produced by particular plants. In the spring, soft colors, such as yellow and chartreuse greens, predominate. As summer comes and goes, these same plants produce colors in the warmer range of gold, bright orange, and reddish orange. With winter come the browns, tans, and beiges. Gather your dyes at different seasons to increase color possibilities.

On the pages that follow are eighteen plants containing dye materials that can be gathered from the wild.

When gathering plants and plant materials from the wild, remember to leave enough for future generations to enjoy and use.

Check the Basic Dyeplant Chart starting on page 5 for additional dyeplants to gather.

Barberry

Berberis species
(see color photo page 124)

Barberry, also called sowberry, is a prickly, deciduous, ornamental and wild shrub, sometimes growing to 10 feet high. It is found naturalized in the eastern United States and parts of Canada. In late spring, barberry blossoms with small, pale yellow, pendulous flowers. Its autumn foliage is bright red with red berries that are sometimes used to make jellies.

Barberry twigs and roots are a good source for a strong yellow dye that has been traditionally used without mordants in European and Scandinavian countries. Native American Indians are known to have used the crushed berries from the barberry bush to color their skin purple.

Barberry is a good dye for silk and makes a range of yellow dyes on wool, linen, and leather.

Bindweed

Convolvulus arvensis

Bindweed, also known as field bindweed or creeping jenny, is a member of the Morning-Glory Family. It is considered to be a garden pest and has been officially labelled a noxious weed by the United States Department of Agriculture. This designation, however, does not keep bindweed from being useful to natural dyers.

Found throughout most of the United States, bindweeds grow easily (too easily!) in waste areas and in cultivated fields. The bindweeds have fleshy roots that sometimes grow as deep as 10 feet. When the roots are broken or chopped up, the plant sends up new plants from each little piece of the root. The plants sprawl along the ground or twine up fences, poles, or any upright in their path.

The flowers resemble that of its tamer cousin, although bindweed blossoms are smaller. Arrowhead-shaped leaves are situated along vines that are strong enough to be used in basketry as binders.

With various mordants, bindweeds make a large range of colors from dull green to khaki green to yellow.

Black walnuts

Juglans nigra

The hulls from black walnuts are popular among natural dyers because of their deep dark brown pigments. Black walnut hulls can be used as an overdye with indigo or logwood to produce black.

Used since ancient times, black walnut hulls produce lightfast dyes even without mordants, although mordants can be used to produce a wider range of hues. The hulls of the white walnut or butternut (*Juglans cinerea*) were used to dye the uniform fabrics worn by Confederate soldiers during the American Civil War. This is how the soldiers came to be known as "butternuts."

For the strongest dye, gather and use the hulls when they are green, or dry them for later use. They make strong dyebaths; several handfuls are enough to dye close to 2 ounces of wool.

To use the hulls for dyeing, soak them overnight in water and then boil for several hours. The longer the hulls are soaked or boiled, the stronger the dyebath will be.

Coltsfoot

Tussilago farfara

Coltsfoot is a wild plant that bears bright yellow flowers in the early spring. If you plant it in your garden, keep an eye on it, because it has a tendency to spread rapidly. It is happiest in dry, sunny spots.

Coltsfoot is used to make an old-fashioned candy stick known as "coltsfoot rock," flavored with oil of anise or dill.

The leaves give a range of greens and yellowish green colors when used with alum and copper.

Dandelion

Taraxacum officinale

The common dandelion is high on my list of favorite "misunderstood plants." Although to some it is simply a weed to be eradicated from the lawn, the *officinale* designation in the plant's botanical name is there for good reason. The dandelion has been used for centuries for both food and medicine. *Taraxacum* is from the Greek words *taraxos* meaning *disorder* and *akos,* meaning *remedy.*

Dandelions are perennials that can grow from 2 to 12 inches tall. The plant grows in fields, waste areas, roadsides, and especially in lawns. The root, which can grow as deep as 18 inches, regenerates itself when broken.

Dandelions are easily grown from seed in the home garden; many garden suppliers carry

these in their catalogs.

The whole dandelion plant can be used in the dyepot — flowers, stems, leaves and roots — to make a range of substantive yellows and yellow-greens. Pick the flowers in full bloom and use for dyeing while still fresh. By the way, the old rumor that dandelion roots yield a magenta dye seems to be just that — a rumor.

Dock

Rumex species

Dock is a common weed found throughout North America. The perennial plant reproduces by seeds and grows at roadsides, in fields, meadows, waste places, and gardens. It has large, coarse, rough leaves with small greenish flowers that turn a darker reddish brown at maturity.

All parts of the plant can be used in the dyepot to make a range of colors from beige to medium brown to green with various mordants.

Elder

Sambucus canadensis

The elder is a fast-growing deciduous shrub, which grows to over 6 feet tall in the wild. The creamy white, fragrant flower clusters that appear are closely followed by dark purple berries that have been used for everything from jellies to wines. These shrubs are fast growers and thrive in a rich, moist, well-drained soil.

The elderberry bush is a treasure chest of colors. The leaves make greens, the bark produces blacks, and the berries make a variety of purple-blue or pinkish beige colors.

Goldenrod

Solidago species

The beautiful golden plumes of goldenrod flowers light up the roadsides during their blooming season in late summer through early fall. They are found in open places throughout the northeastern and north central parts of the United States, as well as in Canada from Newfoundland to Manitoba. Goldenrod is easily grown in the home garden (see chapter 6).

Goldenrod flowers should be used in the dyepot when fresh to make a range of yellows and rusty orange colors with various mordants.

Grape

Vitis species

Many species of wild grapes grow throughout North America, but the leaves and fruits on the wild varieties are much smaller than on cultivated varieties. Grape leaves are useful to produce a range of yellows on wool.

Milkweed

Asclepias syriaca

A perennial plant native to North America, milkweed is found in the wild throughout the eastern United States except along the Gulf Coast, and in Canada from New Brunswick to Saskatchewan.

The fibrous inner layer of the plant was used by Native American Indians to make fishing nets and rope.

The leaves and flowers of milkweed make a range of colors from moss green to yellows or browns.

Mullein

Verbascum thapsus
(see color photo page 126)

Two varieties of mullein can be used for dyeing, great mullein (*V. thapsus*) and moth mullein (*V. blattaria*). Great mullein (also called flannel plant, velvet plant, candlewick plant, feltwort, tinder plant, rag paper, Jacob's staff, beggar's blanket, Adam's flannel, and a multitude of other names) grows to a height of 8 or 9 feet when grown in the wild. Moth mullein is smaller and does not grow over 4 feet high. Mulleins are hardy, sun-loving biennials found growing in the wild in chalky, sandy, or gravelly areas. (For information on growing mullein in your home garden, see chapter 6.)

Leaves and stalks of mullein (fresh or dried) make a range of yellows, golds, and brasses when used with various mordants on wool, silk, cotton, or linen.

Mustard (wild)

Brassica species

A common annual throughout North America, wild mustard is actually considered a serious weed in many areas. It grows in gardens, on cultivated land, and in grain fields. The seeds can live in the soil for many years before they germinate. Mustard blooms in the early spring with bright yellow flowers that produce brilliant shades of yellow on wools.

Nettle (stinging)

Urtica dioica

A common weed, nettle should be gathered during spring or summer. It grows wild throughout most of the United States *except* southern Georgia, most of Florida, and from northwestern Washington through central and southern Texas. You'll find it in waste places, vacant lots, and damp woods; it prefers rich soils.

Nettle has traditionally been used for medicine and food. In Scotland, yarn spun from nettle fibers was used to make household linens.

The whole stinging nettle plant can be used for dyeing. As the season progresses, the colors obtained from its tops change from a creamy beige to a more yellowish color.

Wear gloves when collecting this plant, as the tiny stinging hairs along its stems contain oxalic acid that will sting for hours afterwards.

Oak

Quercus species

You may have heard of the dye called *quercitron*. Quercitron extract is made from the inner bark of the black oak or yellow bark oak. The tannins in all oak barks give good tan dyes that darken with exposure to light and over a period of time.

Collect the bark from felled trees, firewood, or pruned limbs. A range of brown, rosy tan, and beige hues can be produced from various species of oak barks.

To use oak bark for dyeing, see pages 51–52.

Pokeweed

Phytolacca americana

Pokeweed is known by a variety of names, including pokeberry, American spinach, American nightshade, Virginia poke, inkberry, redweed, pigeon berry, bear's grape, pocanbush, and poke salad. American Indians favored pokeweed dye for staining their baskets.

Pokeweed is a perennial herb that grows wild along roadsides throughout most of North America to a height of 5 feet or more. The shiny dark purple berries used for dyeing appear in July through September and give a range of pinks, reds, and reddish browns on wool, silk, cotton or linen.

Pick the berries late in the summer after they have turned a dark purple color. Crushing the berries while they simmer will produce more dye. To use pokeweed dye, see page 51.

Pokeweed can also be grown in your home garden (see chapter 6). Seeds are available from a variety of mail-order herb and seed suppliers.

St.-John's-wort

Hypericum perforatum

Also known as the Herb-of-St.-John's, nits-and-lice, speckled John, and Klamath weed, St.-John's-wort is a perennial that is related to rose-of-Sharon *(H. calycinum)*, a commonly used ornamental ground cover.

Throughout history, St.-John's-wort was used to protect against evil and disease, because it was considered to have magical powers. It has been a popular folk remedy for healing wounds and treating kidney afflictions and nervous disorders.

St.-John's-wort is native to West Asia, Europe, North Africa, and other locations, and has become naturalized in many parts of the world. In North America, the plant ranges throughout the eastern half of the United States all the way to the Pacific coast and is especially prevalent in southern Oregon and northern California. The plant also grows wild north into southern Canada in Quebec and Ontario.

As a dyeplant, St.-John's-wort makes a range of bright yellow colors when used with alum or chrome. It has good lightfastness according to Judy Green (*Natural Dyes from Northwest Plants*). Use the stems, leaves, and fresh flowers of the plant. St.-John's-wort contains tannin, which is at its highest concentration in the plant when the buds are forming right before flowering. The bright yellow blooms, which are almost ¾ inch in diameter, appear from June until September. If older, withered flower heads are used, the resulting color is more of a medium brown.

According to the *Herb and Spice Handbook* published by Frontier Herbs, the flowers of St.-John's-wort may also produce pink dye, but this is its only reference to its use as a pink dye.

St.-John's-wort can also be easily cultivated in the home garden (see chapter 6).

Sumac

Rhus glabra
(see color photo page 128)

Sumac is a perennial shrub or small tree that grows to 20 feet in height. Also known as smooth sumac, mountain sumac, dwarf sumac, and scarlet sumac, it grows throughout the entire United States, as well as into Canada and Mexico. The leaves of the flame-leaf sumac that grow in my area of Texas turn bright red after the first winter freeze. Sumac spreads by seeds or rootstock and prefers dry soils, pastures, and waste areas. The greenish white flowers appear in June or July and turn into the *drupes* (berries).

Sumac berries, stems, twigs, leaves, and bark may be used with various mordants to get shades of brown, yellow, gray, and black.

Note: Don't confuse this plant with poison sumac.

Sumac extract is also available from some suppliers (see chapter 8).

Tomato

Lycopersicon lycopersicum

At the end of the gardening season, gather up all your tomato vines and take them on a detour before composting them. (If you are lucky enough to have a community garden in your area, you might find it to be a good place to scavenge for plant materials such as this at the end of the growing season.) I've found that tomato vines *(before* frost has nipped them) make a pretty, pale greenish yellow on wool or silk if used with alum. Used with no mordant, and in very large quantities, tomato vines make brown to reddish brown colors.

Karen Casselman *(Craft of the Dyer)* also suggests creating a dye with spoiled green tomatoes or those that have been nipped by an early frost.

☕ chapter 6 ☕

Dyes from Your Garden

*W*ouldn't it be handy to be able to walk out your own back door and gather a basket full of lovely flowers for the dyepot? This is possible if you grow your own dyeplants in your home garden. Growing a dyeplant garden can be incorporated into your normal garden activities — you don't have to have several acres of land or give up a lot of room just to grow plants for the dyepot. Many traditional dyeplants, such as indigo, madder, and safflower, also make lovely landscape plants. Many other potential dye plants, such as coreopsis, cosmos, zinnias, and marigolds, are common, easy-to-grow annuals and perennials that also make lovely additions to your landscape or cutting gardens. The flowers can be enjoyed right up until the time that they begin to fade and then plucked one by one and saved for the dyepot.

A garden of potential dye flowers doesn't have to be expensive, either. Lots of these flowers are easily grown from seed or nursery transplants that are available from herb suppli-ers, your local retail nursery, or mail-order nurseries. (See Appendix for source list or *Nature's Dyepot,* which is listed in the bibliography, for an extensive list of suppliers for these seeds and plants.)

This chapter contains basic instructions for growing dye plants. For more information on the basic how-tos of gardening, soil preparation, and propagation and cultivation of these plants, refer to standard gardening books.

It's a good idea to contact your County Agricultural Extension Service agent before planting your dye garden. Some counties in the United States consider some of the more common dyeplants as noxious weeds; you may be penalized if you try to grow them. Woad, for example, is considered a noxious weed in Utah and southern Idaho. Furthermore, some species of barberries are illegal to grow in Canada, as it acts as a host for wheat stem rust. Canadian residents should check with the Canada Department of Agriculture for information on any other illegal plants.

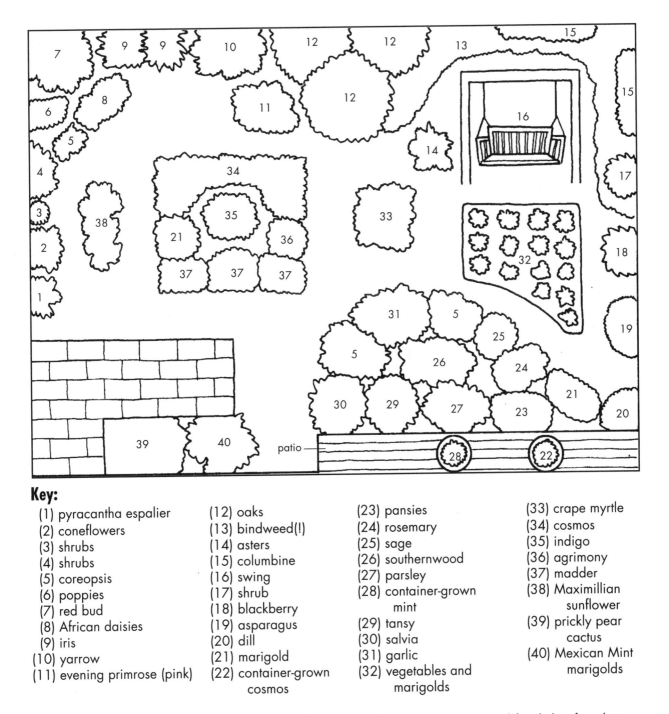

Key:

(1) pyracantha espalier
(2) coneflowers
(3) shrubs
(4) shrubs
(5) coreopsis
(6) poppies
(7) red bud
(8) African daisies
(9) iris
(10) yarrow
(11) evening primrose (pink)

(12) oaks
(13) bindweed(!)
(14) asters
(15) columbine
(16) swing
(17) shrub
(18) blackberry
(19) asparagus
(20) dill
(21) marigold
(22) container-grown
cosmos

(23) pansies
(24) rosemary
(25) sage
(26) southernwood
(27) parsley
(28) container-grown
mint
(29) tansy
(30) salvia
(31) garlic
(32) vegetables and
marigolds

(33) crape myrtle
(34) cosmos
(35) indigo
(36) agrimony
(37) madder
(38) Maximillian
sunflower
(39) prickly pear
cactus
(40) Mexican Mint
marigolds

Many of the plants in my garden are perennials that come back year after year with minimal mainte-nance. Some of the annuals also reseed themselves readily.

This chapter contains descriptions of twenty-four plants that can be used for dyeing. None is difficult to grow in your home garden. Many of them are common herbs — maybe you've never thought to use mint or sage as dyes. Some of them are even considered "weeds" by the unenlightened, but even these homely plants are of value to dryers.

Agrimony

Agrimonia eupatoria

A member of the Rose Family, agrimony is a hardy perennial. It is also known as church steeples, cocklebur, and sticklewort, because of its saw-edged leaves and the little hooklike burrs on the seed pods. Agrimony grows wild in the northern and eastern United States as well as in most of Europe and England,  but it can be easily grown in your home garden, where it makes a nice companion in the rock garden or wildflower border. The plant grows to a height of 1 to 3 feet. It has small yellow blossoms from early summer through early fall.

Although agrimony seed germinates better when sown fresh in the fall than when held over until spring, even in fall seed germination is sporadic. You will have better success if you propagate agrimony by root cuttings in the fall or in early spring when the first shoots begin to sprout. Plants are available from mail-order herb suppliers.

Since agrimony stalks do not fill or branch out, plant them in clumps spaced about 7 inches apart for a better display. Plant *A. eupatoria* in ordinary, well-drained soil with some shade. Fragrant agrimony (*A. odorato*) prefers a more shady location and acid soil.

Harvest the leaves and stems for dyes in the late fall; if harvested earlier, colors tend to a more yellowish cream.

To use agrimony for dyeing, see Dyeing with Herbs and Flowers, page 51.

Bedstraw (lady's)

Galium verum
(see color photo page 125)

A hardy perennial and member of the Madder Family, lady's bedstraw is also known as our-lady's bedstraw, yellow bedstraw, and cradlewort. One legend goes that bedstraw flowers were once white and scentless, but after the newly born Christ child was laid in a manger lined with bedstraw, the flowers turned golden and were instantly fragrant. Lady's bedstraw is also known as cheese rennet, as it was traditionally used to curdle milk for cheesemaking. The flowers were used for coloring cheeses and butter yellow.

A common wild plant throughout both Europe and North America, lady's bedstraw is one of the few native British sources of red dye.

The plant is not difficult to grow in a home garden, but it prefers very deep, loose, sandy soil. Propagate it by sowing fresh seed in the fall, dividing the roots in the spring, or layering it. Its feathery foliage sprawls prostrate along the ground, forming a thick, bright green mat that increases yearly by underground runners. Bedstraw grows as much as 30 inches high. It has tiny, fragrant, four-petalled, golden yellow blossoms that produce a mass of color from late June into August.

The coloring matter in lady's bedstraw is concentrated in the roots, much like madder. To use for dyeing, harvest the roots when the plant is in flower, and use fresh or dried. Remove the thick skin that covers the roots, cut the stripped roots into small pieces, and steep them in warm water overnight. Strain and follow the general procedures for using madder (pages 51–52 and 76). Since the coloring matter in bedstraw is not quite as strong as that in madder, it takes about three times as much bedstraw as madder to obtain the same depth of color.

Chamomile

Chamaemelum nobile

A perennial herb native to Europe, chamomile was used in medieval times as a strewing herb to cover foul smells at public gatherings. In landscaping, it is often used as a ground cover along walkways or paths in partly shady or shady locations. It prefers moist soils.

The plants have threadlike, lacy foliage that forms a spreading mat of aromatic leaves that release their wonderful scent when walked upon. Chamomile grows from 10 to 12 inches high. It bears clusters of small, yellow, daisylike flowers in summer.

Chamomile is easily grown in the home garden by seed, root division, or layering of runners. Space mature plants approximately 6 inches apart.

The flowers are used for dyeing, although because they are quite small, it takes quite a few to make a dyebath. You may wish to purchase dried chamomile in bulk (or in tea bags) at natural food stores or through herbal suppliers.

Chamomile (dyer's)

Anthemis tinctoria

Dyer's chamomile, which should not be confused with *Chamaemelum nobile* (above), is also known as golden marguerite and dyer's marguerite.

This chamomile grows to 2 feet tall; it has light green leaves and golden yellow, daisylike flowers that bloom almost constantly from late summer to early fall. It is happiest in a well-drained, dry, sandy soil in full sun. Perennial dyer's chamomile is hardy to zone 3. It can be propagated by either of two methods. You can sow seeds in spring; they are slow to germinate and can take up to three weeks at 70°F to emerge. You can also propagate by taking cuttings in summer, overwintering them inside, and then planting them outside in the spring when there is no more danger of frost. Thin seeds or set plants 10 inches apart. Once established, chamomile needs little care.

The flowers are used for dyeing. Although all chamomiles can be used in the dyepot, this is the variety best suited for dyeing purposes.

For hints on using chamomile, see Dyeing with Herbs and Flowers, page 51.

Coneflower

Rudbeckia species
(see color photo page 124)

The native North American coneflowers are large daisylike perennials that provide a range of bright colors in the garden from summer until the first frost. Also known as black-eyed Susan, *Rudbeckia hirta* is yellow with an orange or purplish brown base.

All coneflowers are easy to grow in locations with lots of sun or light shade and moist, rich soil. Coneflowers can be grown from seed or from divisions taken in the spring. They grow from 2 to 5 feet high.

Coneflower heads or the whole plant (except roots) make a range of yellow and green colors.

Coreopsis

Coreopsis tinctoria

Coreopsis, like other members of the Sunflower Family, make excellent dye plants that are easy to grow in a home garden. Also known as calliopsis and tick-seed, these annual flowers are available in orange, yellow, and red with contrasting bands of color. Flowers will bloom from July through October if the old flowers are removed.

Coreopsis grows easily from seed sown where it is to grow, and it reseeds readily. These plants grow best in full sun in a moderately moist location. They sometimes reach 36 inches tall.

Flower heads make a range of colors from orange to red-orange. A spoonful of table salt added to the dyebath may deepen the red colors.

Several wild varieties of coreopsis also make good dye plants, and all species yield similar colors. To use coreopsis for dyeing, see Dyeing with Herbs and Flowers, page 51.

Cosmos

Cosmos sulphureus

Cosmos are easy to grow from seed in the home garden. Sow the seed outside where they are to grow, and thin to about 6 inches apart. The plants grow quickly and almost before you know it (from eight to twelve weeks later), they are covered with gossamer, translucent blooms.

In many parts of North America, cosmos reseed easily to make an almost maintenance-free bed of color that will last for years. As a matter of fact, in my Texas garden I was able to get two crops of cosmos flowers the first year I planted them just from my original seedlings and their volunteer offspring that came up in the early fall.

There are many cultivars of cosmos, and they can all be used in the dyepot. The cultivar 'Sunset' blooms in a mass of color varying from deep orange to an orange yellow. The cultivar 'Diablo', which includes many bright yellows, reds, and oranges, is also good for dyeing. Cosmos is also available in bright pinks, whites, and mixtures of deep red, bronzes, and yellows.

Cosmos flowers can be mixed with coreopsis or marigolds to "stretch" the color, if needed. Add ammonia to the cosmos dyebath to bring out and brighten the red hues.

Goldenrod

Solidago canadensis

Although goldenrod is common in the wild, it also makes a handsome garden plant that is easily grown in most soils. Goldenrods are rather tall (up to 36 inches) perennials that thrive in dry locations. They are propagated easily by seed or by cuttings of the creeping rhizomes.

Many people who think that they're allergic to goldenrod are in fact allergic to ragweed instead — the two plants bloom at the same time of the year.

Any part of the plant can be used in the dyepot, but the flower heads give the best yellow hues. For more information, see page 66.

Indigo

Indigofera species
(see color photo page 123)

Several varieties of indigo can be grown in the home garden in warmer climates. Members of the Pea Family, these perennial shrubs make attractive garden plants that often reach 4 or 5 feet in height. Two of the most important species are *Indigofera tinctoria* and *I. suffruticosa*.

Indigo thrives in hot, humid climates, in sunny locations with fertile soil. In cooler climates, the plants can be grown in pots outside during the summer and brought in during the winter if situated in a south window or grown under lights.

Although indigo is tender to frost, the indigo plant in my garden *(I. tinctoria)* has been evergreen even in 30°F weather. The plants do grow more slowly in cooler weather. Rita Buchanan *(A Weaver's Garden)* states that the variety *I. suffruticosa* is more tolerant of cool weather.

Indigo is propagated by seed or root division in the spring. It resents transplanting once established but can be started in a greenhouse over the winter if grown in peat pots to minimize transplant shock. Soak the seeds in warm water overnight before planting to soften the hard seed coat. Plant the seeds ½ inch deep and thin to about a foot apart.

The plants bloom from midsummer through the fall, with small clusters of tiny bronze flowers that develop into brown seed pods.

Rita Buchanan was really the first contemporary author to write about using fresh leaves from the indigo plant *(Indigofera tinctoria)* for dyeing. She has made the whole process easy to understand and cleared away the shroud of mystery surrounding the use of indigo. I have followed her methods, as documented in her classic work, *A Weaver's Garden,* in my own experiments with indigo.

To obtain the indigo pigment from your plants, you must steep the leaves in water at high (not boiling) heat, in the following manner: Cut the leaves just as the plants come into bloom, for this is when they contain the most pigment. Strip the leaves off the branches, pack them into a heat-resistant jar, cover the leaves with water, and screw on a lid. Put the jar into a pan of water and heat it to 160°F for over two hours or until the water turns an amber color. Pour off the amber liquid and use as a dyebath. The solution can be stored at room temperature for quite some time (several months) in tightly capped plastic jugs filled to the top to exclude all air. For information on how to use an indigo dyebath, see pages 89–90.

The solar method for extracting the pigment is to pack the leaves into a container, cover with water (100°F), and cover the container with a lid or clear plastic wrap in order to keep the air out. Put the container in a sunny spot and leave it for about twenty-four hours. Strain out the leaves, and use the resulting liquid for your dyebath. Once the pigment has been extracted, the leaves can be discarded.

For more information on growing, processing, and using a different species of indigo known as Japanese indigo (*Polygonum tinctorium*), see the definitive work on the subject, *Indigo From Seed to Dye* by Dorothy Miller (see Appendix).

Madder

Rubia tinctorum

The roots of the madder plant are an excellent source of red coloring due to the alizarin pigment that resides in between the core of the roots and the outer bark layer. For centuries, madder has been an important commercial product throughout the world. Pliny the Elder wrote of the madder growing near Rome in the first century A.D. In the eighth century, Charlemagne ordered that it be grown on his estates. From the 1400s through the 1600s, Holland was the major madder-producing region in Europe, but by 1782, France had become the major madder grower in Europe. The French Revolution, however, ruined the madder farmers. The fields were later revived by Louis Philippe, who decreed that red caps and trousers were mandatory for his army. In England, madder was used for dyeing the red uniforms of the British army, whose soldiers were known as the "redcoats." Around 1869, however, the production of madder came to almost a complete halt when artificial madder dye was synthesized.

Contemporary weavers and spinners have not let the tradition of using madder completely die out, however, and the cultivation and use of madder is not difficult. Madder can be grown from seeds or plants, and the process can easily be carried on in the home garden.

Ruth Pierce of the Blessing Historical Society in Blessing, Texas, has grown and harvested madder for years. She recommends either germinating the seeds in a greenhouse over the winter or sowing them directly into the garden in spring where they are to remain. Plant the seeds ½ inch deep in well-drained, deeply dug, light, sandy soil in a sunny or lightly shaded area. Water the plants regularly and cultivate to remove weeds. The rough, spiny leaves and stems of madder lie along the ground and should be pinned down from time to time in order to encourage more root growth. Ms. Pierce suggests that the plants can also be grown upright on supports.

Madder plants seem resistant to insects. They are propagated easily by seed, root division, layering, or root cuttings. In the garden, madder spreads rapidly by underground runners. Space mature plants about 10 inches apart.

Madder roots are perennial. The top growth is said to be deciduous, but the plants in my garden have remained evergreen throughout a mild Texas winter where tem-peratures have not fallen below 30°F.

Madder usually flowers in the second year with spikes of tiny yellow flowers resembling stars. Seeds may set during the second year but more likely in the third.

Madder roots should be dug in the fall of the third year. Wash and dry them in the open air or in a warm oven, and then break or cut them into small pieces before they dry out entirely and get too hard. Some dyers suggest separating the various layers of the roots, but I've found that this isn't necessary to get good color. Madder roots should never be boiled; boiling changes the red coloring pigment to brown.

I've had good luck cutting commercially dried madder roots into pieces several inches long with pruning shears and then chopping them up a few at a time in a small food processor. I then soak the roots in warm water overnight. The next day, the water is blood red and ready for the dyepot. The root pieces can be dried and used over several times.

For further information, see Dyeing with Roots and Barks, pages 51–52.

Marigold

Tagetes species
(see color photo page 128)

Marigolds are hardy, trouble-free annuals that are easily grown from seeds sown in early spring. Germination occurs in about fifteen days. Give them a rich soil in a sunny spot, and the plants will bloom from late spring until frost, making more and more flowers as long as the faded flowers are kept picked from the bushes. As you remove the faded flowers, save them in a container until you have enough for a dyebath. It won't take long to gather enough of these, as the dye matter in marigolds is strong.

Marigolds grow from 6 to 40 inches in

height, depending on the cultivar. The yellow, gold, orange, or burgundy flowers can be enjoyed until they fade and then used in the dyepot. Marigolds freely reseed themselves, although they may not come "true to form."

Both fresh and dried marigold flower heads can be used with various mordants to make shades from yellow-orange to gold to dull greens on wools, cottons, and silks. Use less of the dried flower heads than of the fresh. A mixture of marigold and coreopsis makes a good dye.

To use marigolds, see Dyeing with Herbs and Flowers, page 51.

Mint

Mentha species

Mint, a common perennial herb, grows on roadsides and wastelands and is easy to grow in the dyer's garden. Mint grows best in rich soil in shady locations, but will tolerate full sun if watered well. It is easily propagated by division or cutting runners. Mint will run rampant in your garden if not kept in bounds. One way to do this is to plant it in a 5-gallon container sunken in the ground.

All mints have square stems and purplish flowers growing either in whorls or spikes.

There are over thirty species of mints, all of which contain some pigment matter and can be used for dyeing. Granted, mint does not make an outstanding color on wool, but might be useful for a background color in a hooked rug, for example. I've used it to color handmade papers and found that the fresh or dried leaves and stalks give a range of yellow and green colors when used with various mordants.

To dye with mint, see Dyeing with Herbs and Flowers, page 51.

Mullein

Verbascum thapsus or *V. blattaria*

Although mulleins are easy to find growing in the wild, they can also be grown in the home garden and are magnificent specimen plants and great conversation pieces. Great mullein (*V. thapsus*) grows to a height of 8 or 9 feet when grown in the home garden. Moth mullein (*V. blattaria*) does not grow over 4 feet high.

Mulleins thrive in poor, dry soil and are easily grown from seed; germination takes about ten days. Sow seed after all danger of frost has passed where the plant is to grow. Mullein readily reseeds itself. In fact, unless the seed head of great mullein is cut after blooming, the ground will be carpeted with tiny seedlings the following spring. Mulleins bloom in July through August.

Leaves and stalks of mullein (fresh or dried) make a range of yellows, golds, and brasses when used with various mordants on wool, silk, cotton, and linen. For more information, see page 67.

Pokeweed

Phytolacca americana

Pokeweed is a hardy perennial that can be gathered from the wild (see page 67) or grown in your home garden. This perennial shrub makes a striking addition to the landscape with its stems that darken to purplish pink as they age.

Pokeweed is best propagated by seed sown in spring or fall. The plant can also be grown from root cuttings (with shoots attached) in the spring or fall. Plants should be placed from

You can store most fresh dyestuffs for later use, although there is sometimes a slight loss or change of color. Here are some guidelines:

◆ Use flowers either fresh or dried. Some make better colors when used fresh, however, and dandelions and goldenrod should always be used fresh.

◆ Tie materials such as twigs, branches, grasses, leaves, and some flowers in bunches and hang them in an attic, basement, or garage to dry. Keep an eye out for mold or mildew.

◆ Slowly air dry barks and roots, and store them in paper bags until needed.

◆ Store dried nut shells and hulls in paper bags until use.

◆ Dry dyestuffs in a microwave oven if a spell of humid weather makes air drying unrealistic.

◆ Store dyes such as indigo and exotic hardwoods in a dry place in a tightly covered container.

◆ For better color retention, freeze the plants rather than dry them.

---

8 to 10 inches apart.

Pokeweed is not a picky plant and will grow in any soil, sunny or shady, as long as it gets plenty of water or is grown in a damp area.

The pokeberries sometimes do not appear until the second year after planting the seed.

Birds love pokeberries and will readily reseed your pokeweed for you!

Safflower

Carthamus tinctorius

Safflower, also known as false saffron or American saffron, is a member of the Sun-flower Family with spiny leaves and large, showy, deep orange-yellow flower heads. The plant has been grown in dry areas of Europe, Africa, and Asia for hundreds of years for the cooking oil and meal made from the seeds. It has also been traditionally mixed with talcum powder to make a rouge and has been used to color liqueurs, cosmetics, and candies. It is sometimes called *false saffron* because it is used as an inexpensive substitute for saffron as a food coloring.

An annual, safflower blooms in midsummer. Safflower plants grow to 36 inches high and prefer a sunny, well-drained location with plenty of water. Sow safflower seeds where they are to grow in full sun after the last frost in the spring. Safflower is easily grown from seed and will germinate in about two weeks if the temperature is close to 60°F. The seedlings should be thinned to 10 inches apart. Once the plants are established, they can get by with less water.

The safflower blossoms can be used either fresh or dried. When the plants begin to bloom, pick the flowers one by one, spread them to dry and save them until you have enough for a dyebath.

Since the safflower petals contain both red and yellow coloring matter, the process for obtaining the dyes from this plant is a little more complicated than that for other flower blossoms.

Although various authors recommend different methods for extracting these dyes, Rita Buchanan (*A Weaver's Garden*) seems to have the easiest method. She suggests extracting the yellow and red pigments in a two-step process, as follows. To extract the yellow dye, put the petals in a cotton bag, place the bag in a pan, and cover it with cold water. Add 1 cup of vinegar per gallon of water to make a mildly acid solution. Soak the petals overnight and then squeeze the bag to remove all of the yellow dye. This dyebath can be simmered and used just as any other flower dye is used. It makes a range of beautiful yellows on silks, cottons, or wools, with or without mordants.

Next, to extract the red pigment from the petals, rinse them in fresh water until all of the remaining yellow coloring comes out. Squeeze the bag out and put it into another pan, again cover the petals with cold water, and add a tablespoon of ammonia or washing soda to make an alkaline solution. Leave the petals in the water for several hours. Squeeze out the bag once again to express all of the coloring matter, which will now be reddish brown. Discard the petals. Add vinegar to neutralize the dyebath. The water will bubble a bit, and then change from brown to bright red. Use the dyebath as is at room temperature, or heat it to no higher than 150°F. Like madder, the red coloring in safflower will be destroyed if boiled.

Safflower is an excellent dye for silk. It produces a range of colors from pinks to roses to reds. The dried flower heads of safflower are available from some herbal suppliers.

Sage

Salvia officinalis

Common sage (or garden sage) is a hardy perennial herb that grows to 12 inches high with woolly stems and purple, white, or blue blossoms. Best known for its role as the predominant seasoning in the Thanksgiving stuffing, sage also contains some pigment, which can be used as a dye to obtain various shades of yellow.

Sage likes plenty of sun and a sandy, well-limed soil. It can be easily propagated by seed, layering, or cuttings. If grown from seed, germination takes from ten to fourteen days in the spring. Seedlings transplant well and should be grown about 2 feet apart.

To dye with sage, see Dyeing with Herbs and Flowers, page 51.

St.-John's-wort

Hypericum perforatum

An erect shrub growing to approximately 3 feet in height, St.-John's-wort spreads rapidly by runners and reseeds itself easily. The leaves are decorated with small, holelike dots; thus the botanic name *perforatum*. The plant is toxic to livestock.

Many herbal suppliers carry seed for St.-John's-wort. For further information, see page 68.

Sunflower

Helianthus annuus

Sunflowers are large, easy-to-grow annuals that sometimes reach 10 feet high, depending on the variety. Sunflowers need a sunny location, but they are not picky about soil. Sow the seeds in early spring where they are to grow. The seeds need warmth to germinate and will emerge after about five to ten days.

The Maximillian sunflower *(Helianthus maximiliani),* a common prairie plant that can also be cultivated in the home garden, makes an outstanding dyeplant, since the whole length of the stem is covered with yellow blooms. One growing in my garden one summer (a youngster!) reached to over 10 feet tall after being planted in March, and it bloomed off and on until the first frost. At one time I counted over forty flowers blooming at the same time on that one plant.

Sunflowers of all varieties make a range of yellow, orange, and olive brown colors with various mordants.

Tansy

Tanacetum vulgare

Tansy, also known as bitter buttons, is a common herb that grows in the wild and also in home gardens. Tansy has been used for centuries as a medicine and for food, as well as for its insect-repelling properties.

A hardy perennial, tansy grows from 1 to 3 feet high, depending on location. It has fernlike leaves and small, mustard-yellow, buttonlike flowers that resemble round, flat cushions. The flowering tops can be used fresh or dried and stored.

Tansy is easy to grow and thrives in any type of soil, as long as it gets lots of sun and has good drainage. Grow it from seed or from divisions in the spring or fall. The plant spreads quickly, so plant it where it will not take over other plantings.

Tansy flowers, tops, and leaves make a range of yellow and greenish colors. The flowering herb contains tannin, which suggests that it might be a good dye to try on basketry materials, cottons, or linens (see pages 53–54).

Weld

Reseda luteola

Weld, also known as dyer's rocket or dyer's mignonette, is a hardy annual or biennial plant that is easily grown in the home garden. One of the dyes of antiquity, weld has been used since the days of the ancient Romans. It is also probably the most common yellow dye used in England until the age of synthetics. The coloring matter in weld is known as *luteolin.*

The shiny blue-green weld leaves resemble flat rosettes that radiate out as large as 15 inches in diameter during the first year. Weld grows from 4 to 6 feet or more. It blooms in early summer (usually in the second year after planting) with tall spikes of small greenish yellow flowers, and joyfully reseeds itself into all parts of your garden.

Plant weld seeds in early spring in a sandy, well-drained, alkaline soil in a sunny to partially shaded location. Thin the seedlings to from 10 to 12 inches apart when small; they resent transplanting.

The leaves, flowers, and stalks of weld can

be used either fresh or dried to make a strong dyebath that gives a range of lightfast colors from golden yellow to orange to olive green when used with various mordants. During the dye process, the pigment tends to sink to the bottom of the dyepot, so you'll need to stir the bath frequently.

Some older dye books suggest waiting until the plant flowers to harvest it, but Rita Buchanan *(A Weaver's Garden)* writes that the leaves can be harvested several at a time (just like lettuce) for use in dyeing.

You can obtain weld seeds from herb plant and seed suppliers (see Appendix).

Woad

Isatis tinctoria

Woad was used in Europe as a blue dyestuff for centuries before the introduction of East Indian indigo early in the sixteenth century. In America, woad was probably the first blue dyestuff used by the colonists. By the 1700s, when indigo was imported to America from the West Indies, the use of woad diminished.

A biennial, woad can be grown from seed planted in midsummer, or it can be sown in the garden in the late fall to overwinter as seedlings. Germination will occur in about ten days, after which the plants should be thinned to about 8 inches apart. Like weld, woad leaves resemble a circular rosette that can grow from 6 to 18 inches in diameter, depending on location.

Woad contains the same pigment as indigo, *indigotin*. The concentration is smaller, however, so a large quantity of the leaves is required to achieve the depth of blue of indigo. Extract the pigment in the same manner as the indigo pigment (see pages 74–75) and use it in the same way.

Note: Woad is considered to be a noxious weed in some locations. Check with your County Extension Service agent for any restrictions placed on the cultivation of the plant in your area. If you do grow woad, cut the flowers before they have a chance to reseed, and save only a few to replenish your own stock.

Yarrow

Achillea millefolium

Yarrow is a perennial herb that grows wild in the fields and along roadsides throughout North America except in some areas of south Texas and the southwestern states.

Yarrow grows to over 3 feet high and has rough, angular, grayish green stems with feathery, fernlike leaves. The plant blooms from June through September with attractive yellow, white, cream, or pink flower heads, depending on variety, that are bunched in a round, flat-topped cluster. Often mistaken for Queen-Anne's-lace, yarrow blooms later in the season. Yarrow is easily grown from seed, cuttings, or divisions in the home garden.

Yarrow has been known as a medicinal plant since ancient times. It is a good dried flower for arrangements. As a dyeplant, yarrow produces a range of colors from bright yellow to gold to yellowish green.

Zinnia

Zinnia species

Among the easiest garden flowers to grow, zinnias are favorite half-hardy annuals that bloom in bright colors of red, orange, pink, or purple in the summer through the first frost. Zinnias prefer hot weather and lots of water.

Zinnia can be started from seed indoors. It germinates best at around 55°F. Plant the seedlings in individual pots, and after hardening them off, plant them in the garden after all danger of frost is passed and the nights are warm. You can also sow the seeds directly in the garden where they are to grow after all risk of frost has passed. Direct outdoor planting produces stronger, better plants. You can also easily find seedlings at nurseries in the early spring. Seedlings should be planted out or thinned to 12 inches apart. Some varieties of zinnias are susceptible to powdery mildew. This is remedied somewhat by watering the plants from the bottom and not overly soaking the petals.

The many different varieties, colors, and sizes of zinnias may be used for dyeing materials a range of yellow and greenish yellow colors.

🍲 chapter 7 🍲

Dyes from the Grocery Store

All dyes don't have to be gathered from the wild or ordered through the mail. A supply is often as close as your neighborhood grocery store. Coffee, tea, cranberries, lettuce, onion skins, purple cabbage, and turmeric and other spices all make fine dyes for natural fibers. Some are not as lightfast as others, but they are inexpensive, serve as a good introduction to natural dyes, are safe to use with children, and are easy to obtain.

There is one thing to remember about dyeing with foods. Many foods you buy in the grocery store have been colored with synthetic dyes to make them more appealing to consumers. Some of these, such as orange skins and canned vegetables, particularly canned beets, may yield bright, wild colors, but they'll be anything but natural!

Cabbage, purple

Brassica oleracea

Purple cabbage does not make an outstanding color on regular wool yarns, but it is fun to experiment with, and it does make some surprising colors on scraps of unmordanted silk fabrics and exceptionally bright colors on DMC needlepoint wools.

Use two heads of purple cabbage to 4 ounces wool, tied into small skeins. Chop the cabbage and cover with 4 quarts water. Simmer for 1½ hours or until the cabbage leaves look bleached of all color. Strain out the cabbage pieces, and add enough water to cover the mordanted wool. Heat the dye solution and yarn to a simmer, and then maintain this temperature for an hour, occasionally stirring the wool. If possible, let the yarn cool in the dyebath overnight.

Coffee

Coffea arabica

Buy a pound of inexpensive coffee, or collect used coffee grounds in a container in your refrigerator, or dry and store them in a covered container until needed. Powdered instant coffee or leftover coffee (brewed) can also be used as a dye.

Coffees give good tans and beiges on cottons or wools, and can be used to create an "antique" effect on natural muslin. They are fairly lightfast if mordants are used. Leave the fibers in the dyepot for several days to darken the shades.

Cranberry

Vaccinium macrocarpon

Cranberries are scarce in my part of the country most of the year, and when they arrive in the grocery stores in November, they don't last long! If you live in a part of the country where they are more plentiful, however, try experimenting with them in your dyepot. Cranberries produce a range of blues and grays on wools or cottons.

Lettuce and Spinach

Lactuca species and *Spinacia* species

Although some dye book authors claim that lettuce and spinach make fugitive dyes, others, such as Karen Casselman (*Craft of the Dyer*), state that they have had good luck making a range of tan to yellow colors with both spinach and lettuce.

Use canned or frozen spinach (with no added dyes) or garden spinach that has gone to seed. Keep the dyebath at a low simmer, and rinse the fibers in white vinegar before drying.

Onion skins

Allium cepa

Onion skins make a good substantive dye, although the colors are brighter and clearer when used with mordants.

Save your onion skins a little at a time in a mesh bag or open container (they'll mold if covered). If your home onion consumption is low, you might try collecting skins from grocery stores or farmer's markets. It takes surprisingly few of these to dye embroidery threads or needlepoint wools.

Cover the skins with water, bring the mixture to a boil, and simmer for approximately 1 hour or until the skins look bleached of all color. Add well-wetted, premordanted yarns, cotton embroidery floss, or fabrics, and simmer for another hour or until the desired color is achieved. The colors will be darker if the fibers are allowed to cool in the bath overnight. (My mother calls this process "skinny dipping"!)

Yellow onion skins give a variety of lightfast colors on different fibers. They make an effective dyestuff for naturally dyed eggs (see pages 143–144).

Experiment with other types of onion skins, such as purple, or try a mixture of two types of skins.

Nowadays, many grocery store onions are treated by their growers to retard sprouting.

The chemicals that they use can also affect the colors of your dyebath. Another good reason to "grow your own"!

Tea

Thea sinensis

Collect and use leftover teabags, old, stale teas, or fresh tea leaves to make a range of colors from beige to tan to brown. The colors produced depend on the variety of tea used and the strength of the dyebath. Teas can be combined with coffee in the same dyebath to make a stronger solution. As with coffee, an afterbath in vinegar may help to make the colors more lightfast.

Turmeric

Curcuma domestica

Turmeric, a common spice available in the supermarket, is the ground tuber of the turmeric or Indian saffron plant. One of the essential ingredients in Indian curry and also used in Worcestershire sauce, the bright orange turmeric powder has been used traditionally to make a bright yellow dye. The name *curcuma* is derived from the Arabic *kurkum,* meaning *saffron,* a yellow dye.

Although turmeric is a fugitive in some circumstances, it is a substantive dye that gives bright colors on wools, basketry materials, cottons, and silks. It is also a good, clear yellow to mix with other colors when topdyeing. The use of mordants may make turmeric more fast.

♨ chapter 8 ♨

Dyes to Order

lthough we can get hundreds of yellows, browns, beiges, and greens from plants grown in our gardens or gathered from the wild, sources for blues and reds are rarer and may have to be purchased from mail-order suppliers. In addition, some of the more exotic dyestuffs, such as hardwoods like brazilwood or logwood, are not grown in this country and must be imported. These, as well as padauk, koa, mahogany, and quebracho, are available from suppliers listed in the Appendix.

Alkanet

Anchusa tinctoria

Alkanet, a member of the Borage Family, has been used for centuries for its red coloring matter.

Pliny the Elder wrote that *Alkanet tinctoria*, or dyer's alkanet, was used by ancient civilizations for dyeing wool, and

the herbalist Gerard recommended it be "drunke with hot beere," adding that "the Gentlewomen of France do paint their faces with these roots." As a matter of fact, the word "anchusa" comes from the Greek for "paint for the skin." During the Middle Ages, alkanet root was boiled with sweet butter and wine to make a medicinal potion known as "red butter." Native Americans used various alkanets for body paint. It is still used for coloring oils, pomades, medicines, and wines.

The somewhat fugitive red dye is concentrated in the roots and makes reddish to blueish grays.

Annatto

Bixa orellana

Annatto, also known as roucou, achiote, or arnatto, is a shrub that is native to South and Central America. The waxy, fragrant annatto seeds have been used for centuries to produce orange, reddish, and pinkish colors on cottons and silks. Annatto has also been used to color cheeses or butters yellowish orange, and it is still popular today in some Mexican dishes. Although the seeds can be found in larger supermarkets and in local natural food stores (in the bulk section) in some areas, they may have to be ordered by mail.

The annatto pigment comes from the waxy outer covering of the seeds. In the past, this covering was soaked, fermented, macerated, washed, and pressed into cakes or pastes and sold. Fortunately, all of this activity is not necessary to release the orange pigment from the seeds. You can simply cover the seeds with water and bring the bath to a boil. The waxy coating will come off the seeds and coat the sides of the pan with a substance that looks like a melted orange crayon. Allow the bath to stand overnight, or strain out the seeds and use the bath immediately to dye silks, cotton fabrics, and wools various shades of reddish orange.

Brazilwood

Caesalpina echinata or *Haematoxylum brasiletto*

Brazilwood is available as wood chips or sawdust, or in extract form. The extract is prepared from the heartwood of one of two redwood trees, *Caesalpina echinata* or *Hematoxylon brasiletto*. The name brazilwood is derived from the Arabic word *braza*, meaning *bright red*. Brazilwood was once used as an additive to madder baths to deepen the color. Also known as *hypernic,* brazilwood extract is easy to use and goes a long way in making bright, lightfast red and purple shades.

If you are using brazilwood chips or sawdust rather than extract, soak these overnight in warm water before use. I have found that brazilwood chips and sawdust contain a lot of pigment and that they can be dried and reused several times.

Cochineal

Dactylopius coccus

Cochineal comes from the dried and pulverized bodies of a tiny insect that lives on certain cacti that grow in Central and South America, Mexico, and the Canary Islands. Other wild varieties of the insects grow in parts of the United States.

The Spaniards that came to Mexico in 1518 found the natives there dyeing cloth with cochineal. Uninformed, they thought the tiny insects were seeds from a native plant. They shipped the insects back to Spain, and the dye was eventually exported throughout Europe and finally found its way back to the English colonies. By the 1700s, cochineal was one of the staple red dyes, along with madder.

Today, pre-dried ready-to-use cochineal can be purchased in little jars. It makes a range of beautiful reds, pinks, magentas, and fuschias on many fibers with various mordants and assistants.

I have been able to reuse cochineal several times. These little wonders contain lots of pigment, so don't throw them out after using them only once! I usually cover the cochineal dye with water and store it *labelled* in the refrigerator in a covered jar until I want to use it again. Like many red dyes, cochineal is sensitive to heat and should not be boiled excessively.

Cutch

Acacia catechu or *Uncaria gambier*

Cutch is traditionally made from the wood of an acacia tree *(Acacia catechu)* that is native to Burma and India. Some of the commercial cutch extracts sold today, however, are derived from other sources such as gambier *(Uncaria gambier)*.

No matter what the source, cutch makes beautiful, fast, rich browns and tans on wools, silks, and cottons.

Fustic

Chlorophora tinctoria or *Morus tinctoria*

Fustic is prepared from the heartwood of a tree that is a member of the Mulberry Family that grows in the tropics and in Asia. Fustic produces a range of colors from yellow to yellow-orange to gold, depending on the mordants used. The longer the fustic extract is boiled, the more gold the color will be. Fustic is a good underdye with indigo to make greens.

This dye is often called *old fustic* to distinguish it from *young fustic,* a substitute obtained from the twigs of the European smoke tree (*Cotinus coggygria*).

Henna

Lawsonia inermis

Henna is derived from the leaves and young shoots of a small tree native to Egypt, parts of the Middle East, and India. The leaves are dried and ground into a paste. Although the colors vary depending on the type of henna used, basically henna makes a range of browns, yellows, and oranges with various mordants. Reported to be a very fast dye, henna is also used for dyeing the hair and eyebrows.

Hops

Humulus lupulus

The cones (*fuggles*), flowers, vines, and leaves from both wild and cultivated hops plants can be used for dyeing. You can grow your own hops plants or you can order dried hops cones in bulk from herb suppliers, some beermaking suppliers, and even some natural foods stores.

Hops cones contain *lupulin,* a substance used historically for its calming effect. In fact, hops are sometimes used in "sleep pillows" for insomniacs. When hops cones are boiled in a dyepot and lupulin is released into the air, you'll feel like you've stumbled into the field of poppies in the Wizard of Oz! Although some people find the smell a bit strong, it is not harmful. If it bothers you, just make sure you have plenty of ventilation. I happen to find the smell pleasant and earthy. (Maybe I'm just getting used to it; my husband makes his own beer at home!)

Exotic Hardwood Dyes

Most hardwood chips should be soaked overnight before use in the dyepot. In general, sawdust and shavings from hardwoods do not have to be soaked as long as the chips, and it takes less of these materials to obtain a dark color than it does of the chips.

Exotic hardwoods, especially wood chips, can be dried and used several times. I have been able to dry and reuse both brazilwood and logwood chips and slivers several times. In fact, I never have used up all the coloring matter from these two woods. The sawdust and shavings from the woods can also be reused, although not as many times as the larger chips.

Indigo

Indigofera species

For information on growing your own indigo plants, see pages 74–75. You can also buy preprocessed indigo in cake or powder form from mail-order suppliers.

Indigo is one of the few naturally occurring blue dyes. Indigo-dyed textiles and fibers have been found in the tombs of the Pharaohs, and indigo use dates back to at least 2500 B.C. In Asia, indigo has been known and used as a cosmetic dye for more than 4,000 years.

Indigo is unusual in that it is fast to both light and water and needs no mordant. I've used it successfully on embroidery and weaving wools as well as on cotton embroidery flosses and on cotton and wool fabrics.

Dyeing with indigo has a sort of mystique associated with it. Perhaps this is because there are hundreds of different indigo recipes. Sometimes beginning dyers shy away from using indigo at home because it seems to be a long, confusing, complicated process. It's not really that mysterious when you understand what actually is happening.

Many of the historical recipes for indigo vats recommend using such substances as urine (urea), lye, sodium hydrosulfite, copperas, ammonia, and lime water. In fact, these dyers probably simply used whatever was on hand at the time.

Indigo is insoluble in water, so it must be acted on chemically and changed temporarily in order for it to release its blue pigment. This chemical process is called *reduction* and results in a soluble, colorless substance called *indigo white*. The textile is dipped into the vat to become saturated with the indigo white. When it is removed from the vat and exposed to air, the pigment in indigo becomes oxidized and turns blue on the fiber.

The most common indigo reduction recipes use lye and ammonia. After driving all over town looking unsuccessfully for plain lye, I decided to use an alternative recipe, one that uses a combination of Boraxo (washing soda) and Rit Color Remover, which is mostly sodium hydrosulfite. This is a fairly fast, easy method for making a small indigo vat that will dye more than 1 pound of yarn a deep, dark blue and subsequent yarns in lighter shades.

Hydrosulfite/Washing Soda Method

If you have indigo chunks, use a mortar and pestle or a wooden spoon on a hard surface to first break them up into a powder. Indigo-dyeing is messy; wear rubber gloves and an apron over your clothes (unless you want permanently blue shirts and pants). You will need the following:

1 ounce washing soda (Boraxo)
½-ounce indigo powder (which can dye as much as 1 pound yarn)
2 ounces sodium hydrosulfite (1 package Rit Color Remover or Spectralite)
Various jars — 1 gallon, 1 quart, 1 pint, and smaller
Thermometer

1. Mix the washing soda with warm water in a quart jar. Stir until the soda is totally dissolved.
2. If you are using indigo chunks, put the powder into a small jar and add enough warm water to make a solution that is almost the consistency of ink. Make sure that the indigo is well dissolved, with no remaining lumps. If you are using pigment extracted from leaves you have gathered, proceed using that liquid.
3. Pour both mixtures into the gallon jar and fill to ¾ full with hot water (approximately 120°–130°F, but not over 140°F). This indigo vat recipe seems to do best when around 130°F.
4. This mixture is your indigo stock solution. Pour one-half of the mixture into another jar

and reserve for future dyeing projects. The remaining dye will be your indigo vat. (Although the stock solution can be used as is for dyeing, it contains an excess of dye which will cause *crocking*, or rubbing off, of the dye later.)

5. Fill a pint jar with warm water and sprinkle in 1 ounce of the sodium hydrosulfite. Stir until it is dissolved.

6. Pour one-half of this solution into the indigo vat, and stir gently to avoid splashing. Tightly cap the jar with the remaining sodium hydrosulfite solution and label. Reserve for later use.

7. Let the vat stand for approximately 30 minutes. The liquid should turn a yellowish green color. Drop in a small skein or length of well-wetted yarn to test the vat. Stir the yarn around (gently!) for a few moments. Pull it out and squeeze out excess dye. The yarn should be a greenish color, which will gradually turn to blue when it comes in contact with the air. The color will continue to develop over a period of time. Continue to dye yarns and/or fabrics (always well-wetted) in this manner.

Note: There will be some sediment in the bottom of the vat. Try not to let the yarns, especially cotton or wool fabrics, sit in this sediment or they will have darker blue blotches on them where they came in contact with the sediment.

When adding or taking yarn out of the vat, try not to splash. Splashing causes air to enter the vat. If the water in the vat turns back to blue, there is too much air in the solution. Add more sodium hydrosulfite solution, stir gently, and wait 10–15 minutes. The vat should turn back to its greenish yellow color, and you can continue dyeing.

To get darker blue shades on yarn or fabric, re-wet the fiber and add it to the vat. Leave it in for a few minutes, gently stirring occasionally. Take it out, air, and let the color develop.

Repeat this process until the desired depth of color is achieved.

After a while, the indigo in the vat will become depleted. At this time, add some of the reserved indigo stock solution, add more sodium hydrosulfite, place the vat in a container of hot water, stir gently, and wait 15–30 minutes until the vat turns greenish yellow again.

I have had lots of fun using my indigo vat to overdye other colors to produce even more colors. I've used indigo as an overdye with yellow-dyed yarns to get some nice green colors, and I've overdyed reds to get purples. Turmeric-dyed wool briefly dipped into the vat produces a dark forest green. Cochineal overdyed with indigo makes a beautiful royal purple, and madder overdyed with indigo, a dark, deep burgundy color. (Also see Overdyeing, pages 55–56.)

Logwood

Haematoxylum campechianum

Logwood is prepared from the heartwood of a tree that grows in Central and South America and in the West Indies. In use for centuries, logwood found its way into the American colonies by 1671. Logwood was still used commercially to dye silk and wools even after the invention of synthetic dyestuffs in 1856. Sometimes called *Campeachy wood dye*, logwood yields intense blues, bluish purples, and lavenders on various fibers with various mordants. The coloring matter in logwood is highly concentrated — a little goes a long way.

Madder

Rubia tinctorum

Madder can be grown in your home garden (see chapter 6), or the dried roots can be ordered from a number of mail-order suppliers.

As previously stated, madder roots should be cut into small pieces, soaked, and simmered — never boiled! The pieces can be dried and reused several times before all of the pigment is depleted. For more information, see pages 51–52 and 75–76.

Osage orange

Maclura pomifera

Osage orange is also known as *bodark* or *bois d'arc,* a reference to the fact that Native Americans once used the wood for bowmaking.

The extract is made from a tree that is a member of the Mulberry Family and that grows wild in Texas, Oklahoma, and Arkansas. The yellow fruit of the osage orange tree looks much like a fluorescent-green orange when unripe, but it is not edible. As children, we used to call these *horse apples.*

The heartwood of the tree, which is extremely hard, makes a fast yellow dye when boiled in water. It is best to buy this dye material in extract form because it is so difficult to cut the wood.

Osage orange makes a range of lightfast, bright yellows similar to fustic, but more brilliant.

Sumac

Rhus glabra

Although sumac may be gathered from the wild or grown in a home garden, it is also available from suppliers in an easy-to-use extract form. Sumac is high in natural tannin and yields colors in the yellow to tan to brown range. Sumac can be used both as a dye and as an additive to mordant cotton. (Also see information on page 68.)

— PART III ◆

Projects Using Natural Dyes on Natural Fibers

Natural dyes are not just for woolen yarns. Stitchers, rugmakers, quilters, feltmakers, and other fiber artists can take advantage of these beautiful natural colors in their projects. The projects included here — a needlepoint pillow, a crocheted baby blanket and pillow, counted cross-stitch greeting cards, a small wool tapestry, a sewn-wool rug, a cotton wall quilt, a felted purse, a splint basket, a cornhusk doll and wreath, and handmade notepapers made from recycled fibers — all use naturally dyed fibers. Small pieces of cotton fabric, strips of wool, and skeins of embroidery floss can be premordanted and thrown into a ready dyepot to be saved and used later for a quilt, rug, or embroidery project. If you have always used your naturally dyed yarns for knitting or weaving, try working a needlepoint project with them! Or, make a doll or wall quilt with naturally dyed cottons. I guarantee that once you get bitten by the natural dyeing "bug" (and I don't mean cochineal!) that you'll never want to stop.

Around-the-World Needlepoint Pillow

This design is based on a traditional around-the-world quilt pattern worked around a basic grid of small squares. The pattern can easily be enlarged, if you like, by adding additional rows of blocks around the center design. To widen the border, work straight

rows of stitching around the edge of the piece in the same or another color.

I used DMC Floralia yarn in the sample project (page 123), but any high-quality needlepoint wool can be used. For the backing, I used skirtweight wool dyed purple with logwood; heavyweight dyed silk or cotton canvas could be used instead.

Working the Pattern

Follow the diagram (on page 97) for placement of colors.

Work from right to left in continental stitch; all stitches should slant to the right.

Continental stitch

Work each of the small blocks of the central pattern over six spaces and down six spaces to make a total of thirty-six stitches per block. Start with the center square. Next, work the four blocks adjacent to the center square. Continue in this manner, finishing one color before going on to the next, until the entire piece is filled in.

To make colors 6, 8, 10, and 12, take a length of each of the colors indicated on the chart and pull apart the 2-ply yarn. Thread one strand of each color together in the needle. This gives an interesting tweedy effect, especially with dyed yarns.

After finishing the design, carefully check for any skipped stitches before blocking.

Blocking

Because of the tension of the wool pulling against the canvas, the finished piece of needlepoint will most likely have stretched into a diamond shape. The piece must be blocked to form a perfect square before it can be made into a pillow.

A piece of board covered with plastic makes a good blocking surface. On the board, make marks for four squared corners according to the desired measurements of your piece. Tack down one corner of the needlework, and wet the piece with a sponge dipped in warm water and squeezed out until barely damp. Stretch the opposite corner out to the opposite corner mark, and tack it to the board. Working around the four sides of the piece, place tacks every 1–1½ inches, stretching and sponging the canvas as you go. Do not overly wet the needlepoint. Use a barely wet sponge, and add only as much water as needed to stretch the piece. The sample wasn't difficult to stretch, even though it was barely damp.

Place the needlepoint where it will get good air circulation and leave it in position

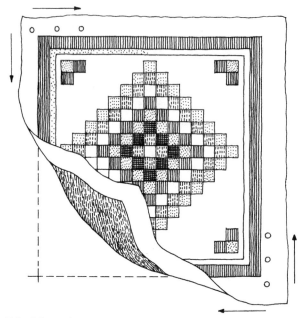

Blocking the needlepoint

on the board until it is dry. Depending on the weather, it should dry completely within a couple of days.

Making the Pillow

1. Trim the needlepoint backing to within 1 inch from the worked design. If the canvas starts ravelling, zig-zag around the four edges to stabilize it until sewn.
2. Pin the needlepoint piece to the backing fabric, right sides together.
3. Sew around all four sides, leaving approximately 3 inches unsewn for turning. Make sure to stitch as close as possible to the worked area.

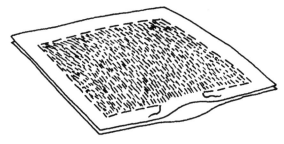

Stitching needlepoint to backing

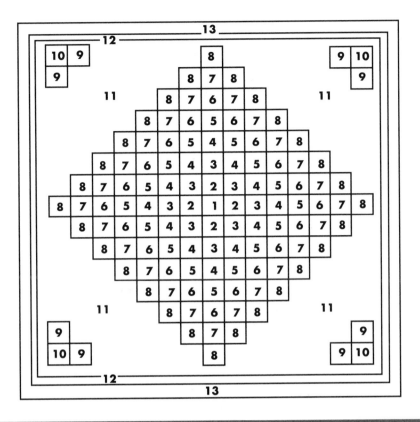

COLOR KEY AND YARDAGE CHART

Color #	Color	Dye Material	Yardage (approx.)
1	Light pink	Purple cabbage	15 inches
2	Medium purple	Logwood	2 yards
3	Dark purple	Logwood and baking soda rinse	3½ yards
4	Light blue	Indigo	5 yards
5	Dark blue	Indigo	7 yards
6	Light pink and burgundy	One strand dyed with brazilwood and baking soda rinse plied with a strand dyed with madder overdyed with indigo	8½ yards
7	Teal blue	Turmeric and indigo	10 yards
8	Blue and red	One strand dyed with indigo plied with a strand dyed with cochineal	11½ yards
9	Dark blue	Indigo	4 yards
10	Light pink and dark blue	One strand dyed with indigo plied with a strand dyed with purple cabbage	2 yards
11	Medium blue	Indigo	42 yards
12	Purple and pink	One strand dyed with purple cabbage plied with a strand dyed with logwood	10 yards
13	Purple	Two shades of logwood plied together	20 yards

4. Trim seams to ½ inch and turn the pillow right side out.
5. Stuff the pillow with polyester fiberfill or batting.

Stuffing the pillow

6. Use matching thread to slipstitch the opening closed.

OPTIONAL:

◆ Run decorative cord or piping around all four sides of the pillow.
◆ Add tassels at each of the four corners. This is a good way to use up short strands of matching leftover yarns.

Matching Needlepoint Yarns

If you dye two colors that are very similar in hue, but not quite matching, separate strands from each dyelot, and use one strand from each together in your needle. Slight variation will not be noticeable in the finished piece.

Baby's First Garden Crocheted Blanket and Pillow

This colorful, cozy wool blanket consists of traditional crocheted granny squares. The sample (shown on page 125) is approximately 26" x 31". Matching pillow is 9" x 12". You could use a variety of colors, as in the sample projects, or limit your color scheme to two or three contrasting or monochromatic hues.

▬ Materials ▬

Naturally dyed medium-weight 2-ply wool yarns:

- ◆ Approximately 8 ounces of a light color (or white) for borders and centers of squares
- ◆ Approximately 16 ounces of various dyed colors of your choice for squares and dark borders

Size D crochet hook, or size required for gauge

Additional 1-ply light-colored yarn and a large tapestry needle for joining the squares

Wool or cotton fabric for pillow (dyed or natural color), two pieces measuring 10" x 13" each

Polyester fiberfill or wool or cotton batting, enough for a 9" x 12" pillow

---

SAMPLE PROJECT COLORS

DYE MATERIAL	MORDANT	COLOR
Brazilwood	Alum/cream of tartar	Reddish brick
Brazilwood exhaust bath	Alum/cream of tartar	Light pinkish red
Logwood	Alum/cream of tartar	Purple
Logwood	Alum/cream of tartar + baking soda rinse	Dark purplish blue
Osage orange	Alum/cream of tartar	Greenish yellow
Annatto	Alum/cream of tartar	Light gold
Marigold and coreopsis	Alum/cream of tartar	Bright yellow
Red cabbage	Alum/cream of tartar	Light tan

The wool fabric for the pillow was dyed with cochineal.

GAUGE: 4-ROUND SQUARE APPROXIMATELY
3¾" x 3¾"

Granny Square pattern

1. With light color, chain 4; join with slip stitch to make a ring. For Round 1: Chain 3 (counts as 1 double crochet) 2 dc in center of ring. * Chain 2, 3 dc in center of ring, repeat from * three times. Chain 2, join in third chain of beginning chain-3 with a slip stitch. End first color.

2. For Round 2, make a slip knot on hook with second color of your choice. Join second color with a slip stitch in any chain-2 space (this is a corner space). Chain 3, 2 dc in same space. Chain 2, 3 dc again in same space. * In next chain-2 space, do (3 dc, chain 2, 3 dc); repeat from * two times. Join with a slip stitch in third chain of beginning chain-3. End second color.

3. For Round 3, join third color of your choice as before in any chain-2 space. (Chain 3, 2 dc, chain 2, 3 dc) all in same space. Between next two 3-dc sets, do 3 dc for side of square. * (3 dc, chain 2, 3 dc) all in next chain-2 space for corner. 3 dc between next two 3-dc sets for side. Repeat from * twice. Join with a slip stitch in third chain of beginning chain-3. End third color.

4. For Round 4, join light (or dark) color again as before in any chain-2 corner space. (Chain 3, 2 hdc, chain 2, 3 hdc) in same space. * (3 hdc between next two 3-dc sets) two times for side. (3 hdc, chain 2, 3 hdc) all in next chain-2 space for corner. Repeat from * two times. (3 hdc between next two 3-dc sets) two times for side. Join with slip stitch in third chain of beginning chain-3. End fourth color.

Crocheting the Squares

Using the traditional Granny Square crochet pattern, make sixty-two squares, working round 1 with a light color (or white) and rounds 2 and 3 with colors of your choice. Work round 4 with light color (or white) again on thirty-eight of the squares. On the remaining twenty-four squares work round 4 with a dark color of your choice.

Six of the squares with a light-colored round 4 will be used for the pillow.

Weave any loose threads into squares.

Assembling the Blanket

To assemble squares, arrange the blocks according to the diagram below, with seven across the width of the blanket and eight down the length. With light-colored yarn,

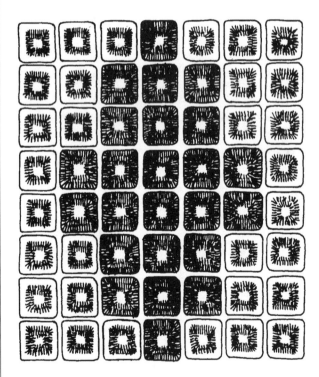

Assembly diagram

use an overcast stitch to sew the squares together. Work on the wrong side, picking up top back loops only. Do not pull the stitches too tightly.

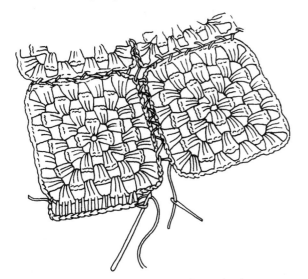

Stitching squares together and crocheting border

For border, attach dark-colored yarn to any corner. Chain 3 for first dc, work 1 more dc, chain 2, 2 dc in same space (4 dc). Continue with 1 dc in each hdc of previous row. Make 2 dc in each chain-2 space around.

Continue this pattern all the way around each of the four sides with 2 dc, chain 2, 2 dc in each corner. Join with slip stitch to first dc at beginning of border. This makes a slightly wavy border that may be made wider by repeating the above sequence. Yarn colors can be alternated in each of these rows if desired.

Assembling the Pillow

Join the remaining six light-bordered squares, and crochet a border using dark-colored yarn as for the blanket. In the sample project, the crocheted piece is simply tacked onto the top of a cotton pillow. To make the pillow, place the two pillow pieces together with right sides facing. Sew around all four sides of the fabric, taking a ½-inch seam. Leave an opening large enough so that the fabric can be turned right side out and filled.

Turn the fabric right side out, and press it. Stuff with polyester fiberfill or cotton or wool batting. Slipstitch the opening closed.

Securely fasten the crocheted block onto the top of the pillow, tacking it down at all four corners and along each side in several places.

Counted Cross-Stitch
Dye Plant Notecards

You will have leftover threads from this project. It is easier to dye an entire skein of embroidery floss at one time than it is to cut it into smaller lengths. If you wish, divide one skein in half and use one half for the yellow colors and one half for the greens. For sample project, see page 124.

The symbols on the stitch diagram correspond to the symbols and colors listed on the color key. Because these are naturally dyed threads, your colors will not exactly match mine, but the project can be successfully worked with similar shades or tints.

You may wish to display these cross-stitch pieces in small frames of your choice, instead of using them as notecards.

See the Appendix for addresses of suppliers of greeting cards.

Materials

No. 24 tapestry needle

Small embroidery hoop

Aida cloth, 100 percent cotton, 11-count, ivory — three small pieces, each at least 6" x 8", or large enough to fit in hoop

Six skeins of embroidery floss, naturally dyed

Greeting cards with cut-outs for cross-stitch

Double-sided transparent tape

Tips for Professional-Looking Cross-Stitch

◆ Do not knot the end of the floss in the needle. Instead, hold the free end of the thread on the back of the work until you have made the first few stitches.
◆ To end a color, weave floss under a few stitches on the back before cutting.
◆ You may carry a color on the back of the fabric from one area of the design to another, but do not go too far, as long carries tend to pucker the fabric.

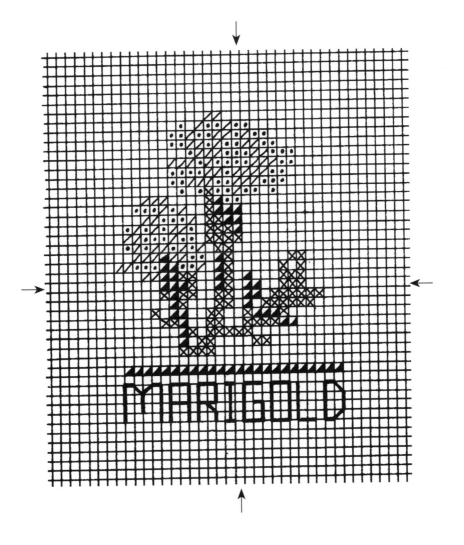

FLOSS COLOR KEY

COLOR	DYE MATERIAL	SYMBOL
Tan	Koa	◹
Light green	Turmeric and indigo	◪
Dark green	Turmeric and indigo	⊠
Yellow	Osage orange	⊙
Red-orange	Madder	⊙

1. Overcast or tape Aida cloth edges to keep them from raveling. To find center of cloth, fold fabric in half horizontally and then vertically. Mark the center with a temporary stitch. The center of each stitch diagram is marked with arrows. Put cloth in embroidery hoop and adjust so that fabric is taut.

2. Cut a piece of floss into 18-inch lengths. Separate lengths into 3 strands each. Refer to the stitch diagram to work the cross-stitch portion of the design. Be sure that all of the bottom stitches of each X slant in one direction and all of the top stitches slant in the opposite direction.

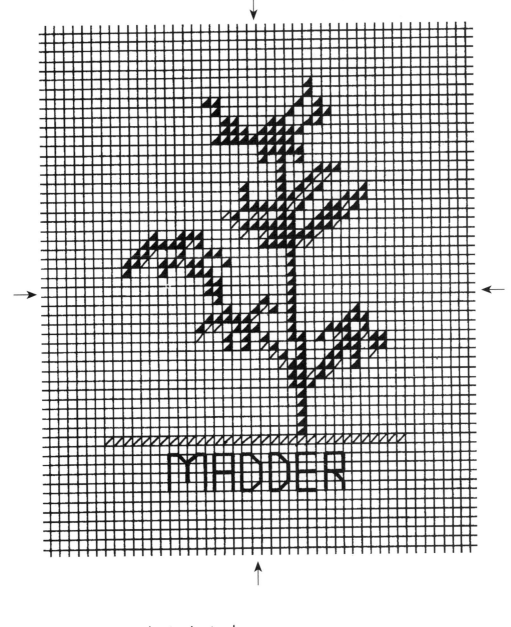

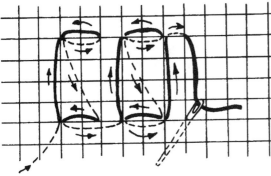

Straight stitch for lettering

3. Work the letters that make up the names of the plants in plain straight stitch, also using three strands of floss (see illustration at the left).

4. When designs are completed, press on the wrong side of the fabric, using a pressing cloth.

5. Use double-sided tape to mount cross-stitch pieces in greeting cards.

Woven Wool Tapestry

This little tapestry (approximately 5" x 5") will serve as an introduction both to tapestry weaving and to using natural-dyed yarns in weaving. It requires three techniques — weaving bands of different colors, using a *cartoon* (see Some Weaving Terminology box) to weave a central motif, and using two colors in the same row — all of which are applicable to larger tapestry projects. In the sample shown on page 123, the blue yarns were dyed with indigo, the yellow were dyed with a mixture of osage orange and onion skins, and the pink, with cochineal.

Some Weaving Terminology

Beater. A tool used to beat the weft firmly and evenly against the already woven section of cloth

Cartoon. An actual-size pattern used in tapestry weaving

Shot. The passage of a weft thread across the warp threads

Weft. The threads that are woven across the warp threads to form cloth

Warp. The threads that run lengthwise on the loom

Materials

Harrisville Friendly Lap Loom or other frame loom

Warp: cotton rug warp (8/4 at 1,600 yards per pound)

Weft: two-ply, natural-dyed wool yarns (knitting worsted or a bit heavier at about 1,000 yards per pound)

Several yards of scrap yarn for weaving headings

Large tapestry needle

Beater (a table fork or a tapestry beater)

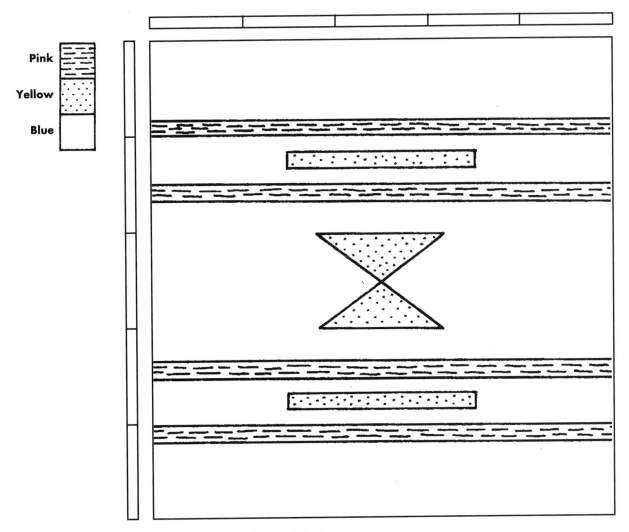

Pattern for tapestry (actual size)

1. To make the cartoon, trace or photocopy the pattern on a piece of sturdy paper.
2. Warp the loom, using four warp ends per inch. Make the tension tight and even. You will need twenty warp ends for this 5" x 5" weaving.
3. Using a large tapestry needle, weave several rows with scrap yarn until the warp yarns are evenly spaced and you have a solid "header" against which to beat the first few rows of the pattern.

4. With the blue weft yarn, plain weave to fill the first section on the cartoon. (To *plain weave*, take the weft yarn over and under adjacent warps on one row, and under and over those warps on the second row, as shown on page 108.) Take care to *bubble* the weft across the width of the warp threads, so as not to pull in the sides of the weaving. The weft yarn should completely cover the warp yarn. After each row, beat the yarn down snugly against

the previous row. Hold the cartoon against the bottom of the warp to check your progress. End the section of blue by cutting the yarn and leaving about 1 inch to take around the outer warp thread and back through the same sequence of warp threads that it travelled in the last row.

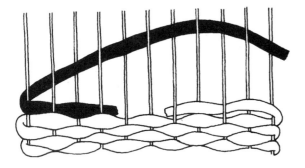

Plain weave, showing how to end one color and begin another, and how to bubble weft

5. Weave the band of pink. Begin on the opposite side from where you ended the blue weft, weaving in a 1-inch end of pink weft in the same sequence as the first pink row, as shown above. Weave until the pink band matches the cartoon. End the band as in step 4.
6. Weave the next section of blue.
7. Weave the section of blue and yellow, using the meet-and-separate technique shown below. Note that you must use

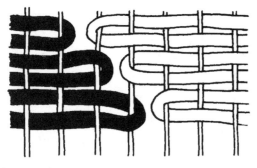

Meet-and-separate weaving

three strands of yarn in this step: two strands of blue and one strand of yellow.

8. Continue to weave, following the cartoon, until you reach the central motif. Weave the central motif using the same meet-and-separate technique used in step 7.
9. Continue the weaving until you complete the pattern.
10. Weave five or six rows with scrap yarn, and beat down firmly.
11. Leaving as much warp as possible, cut the first two warp threads at the top of the loom, pull them out of the heading, and tie them together with a square knot. Continue across the width of the weaving, until all the top warps are tied together. Do the same for the bottom warp threads.

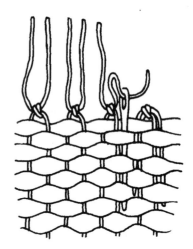

Weaving knotted warps back into woven piece

12. Use a tapestry needle to weave the ends into the woven piece as shown.

Sewn-Wool Fabric Rug

When I first planned the projects to include in this book, I wanted to make a hooked rug with naturally dyed wool strips. After struggling for a period of several months, however (and talking to numerous people who started but *never* finished a hooked rug!), I decided to include an easier, faster project for those dyed wool fabrics — one that would definitely get finished! I sewed this fun rug (about 24" x 30") on the sewing machine, and it took only a little over three days (sewing part-time) to complete. The colors in the design can easily be changed to suit your decor or to use up dyed wool fabrics that you have on hand. Use a rotary cutter and cutting mat to make the cutting go quickly and painlessly. The sample rug (page 126) uses approximately 4 yards of 60-inch-wide fabric.

Experiment — try one in cotton!

SQUARES TO CUT

COLOR	DYE	NUMBER (APPROXIMATE)
Blue	Indigo	760
Lavender	Logwood	115
Pink	Cochineal	110
Yellow	Hops	100
Purple	Logwood	80
Green	Turmeric + indigo	60

Materials

Dyed skirt-weight wool, cut into 2" x 2" squares

Heavy cotton fabric or canvas for backing (approximately 30" x 36")

Carpet thread and large needle

1. With black permanent marker, draw stitching guidelines, ½ inch apart, lengthwise on rug backing fabric. Use another color permanent marker to transfer the design to the center of the rug backing. (See page 147 for tips on how to enlarge patterns.)

Gauge: 1 square = 1 inch

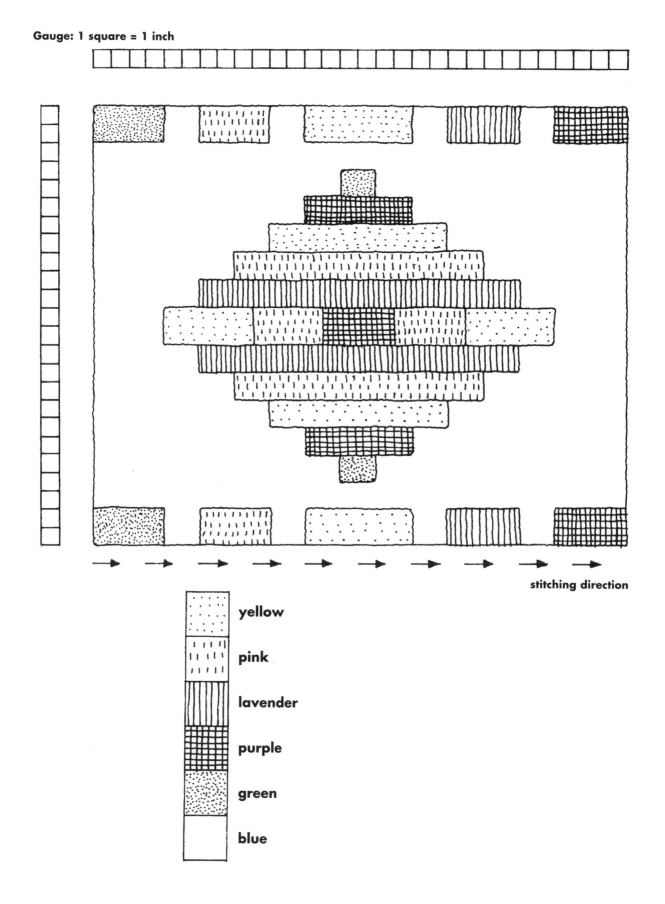

stitching direction

yellow

pink

lavender

purple

green

blue

2. Each tuft of the rug is made by folding a 2" x 2" square of fabric into thirds and sewing it to the backing in the following manner: Fold the outer edges of each square into the center. Place the folded piece on the backing, as shown below, and stitch across the center. The squares should be sewn on in straight lines in rows approximately ½ inch apart. Start in the middle of the rug and work your way out toward the ends, filling sections as indi-

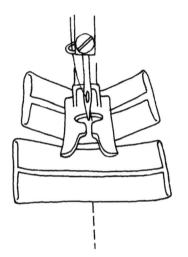

Stitching folded wool squares along guideline

cated on the pattern. The rug gets heavy and needs support while being sewn.

3. When all of the rug backing is filled with squares, turn under the hems all the way around the rug, and slipstitch in place using the carpet thread and large needle. Miter the corners, as shown below.

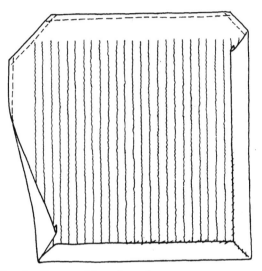

Back of rug with mitered corners

4. Trim stray threads and any squares that are obviously higher than the others.

Quilted Cotton Wall Hanging

This small cotton wall quilt (page 124; approximately 20" x 20"), based on the "sew-before-you-cut" quilting method, goes together easily and swiftly. I used cotton fabric dyed with logwood, madder, cochineal, osage orange, indigo, turmeric, marigold, coffee, and purple onion skins for the solid-color pieces, and a paste-resist technique and a logwood dyebath for a few accent squares.

This quilt may also be made of wool fabric.

Materials

Dyed cotton fabrics (less than 2 yards)

Rotary cutter and mat

Matching and contrasting threads

Rice flour, for paste resist (available at Oriental markets)

Cotton quilt batting (approximately 21" x 21")

Piece of plain (or dyed) cotton fabric for backing (21" x 21")

Quilt Top

1. From the dyed cotton fabric, cut 1½" x 30" strips.
2. Using a ¼-inch seam, sew five of the strips together to make one long block of strips. (Offset the strips as shown below, to avoid waste.)

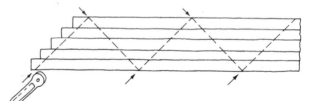

Cutting lines for stitched strips

3. Use a rotary cutter and a straight-edge ruler to cut six triangles from the block of strips. Make each side 6 inches.
4. From solid-color fabric, cut four triangles, also with 6-inch sides.
5. Using a ¼-inch seam, sew each of the four solid-colored triangles to a pieced triangle to form four squares. Each square should measure approximately 5½ inches. Sew

the remaining two pieced triangles together to form a fifth square.

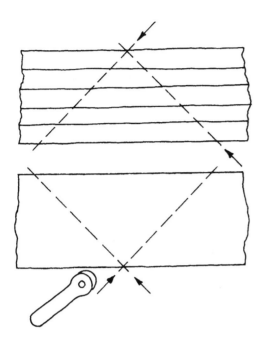

Putting together the pieced and solid-color triangles

6. Cut four 5½-inch squares from the paste-resist treated fabric. (See Simple Paste-Resist Technique, at the right.)
7. Follow the pattern shown below at the right to assemble the quilt top.

Quilt Border

8. For the quilt borders, cut four pieces of cotton fabric, 2½" x 19".
9. Take two of the border pieces, and sew one to each side of the quilt top.
10. Cut four corner squares, 2¼" x 2¼".
11. Stitch the corner pieces to each end of the remaining border pieces. Stitch these borders to the quilt top. (See illustration at right.)

Simple Paste-Resist Technique

1. Premordant a piece of cotton fabric.
2. Dissolve ½ cup of rice flour in warm water to make a thin paste.
3. Stir to remove as many lumps as possible, or put mixture into a jar and shake vigorously. Strain out any lumps.
4. Dip a large paintbrush into the flour-water mixture and "paint" designs onto the premordanted fabric. Leave some areas blank. Use free-hand squiggles, lines, dots, or specific designs.
5. Let the flour dry thoroughly.
6. Wet the fabric slightly with cold water, taking care not to disturb the resist. You can do this by quickly dipping the fabric into a pan of water or by spraying it with a plant mister.
7. Carefully dip the fabric into a strong, cooled dyebath of logwood, indigo, or Brazilwood and leave for a few minutes.
8. Remove the fabric and hang to dry. After the fabric is dry, rinse it under warm water until the excess dye and resist are removed.
9. Soak the fabric in cold salt water for several minutes. Remove and hang to dry. Press fabric and use in quilt project.

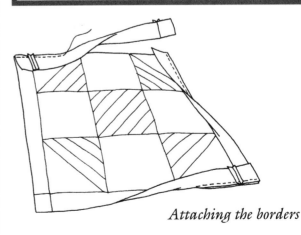

Attaching the borders

Batting and Backing

12. Cut batting to same size as quilt top. Pin batting to wrong side of quilt top.
13. Pin quilt backing to right side of quilt top.
14. Using a ½-inch seam allowance, sew around the perimeter of quilt, leaving approximately 6 inches open for turning.
15. Remove all pins; trim seams and stray threads. Trim batting as close to seam as possible.
16. Turn quilt right side out. Make sure corners are well turned.
17. Iron front and back of quilt.
18. Turn in opening, press and slipstitch closed.
19. Machine quilt ¼ inch away from all seams on top of the quilt. Trim stray threads and press.

Batik on Silk

Materials

Piece of mordanted 100 percent silk fabric (18" x 22")

Wooden frame about 12" x 15" and push pins

Old electric skillet with thermostat or double boiler with thermometer

Wax (¼ beeswax to ¾ paraffin, if possible)

Baking soda

Soft natural-bristle paint brushes (inexpensive ones are fine)

Pan of warm water

Lukewarm osage orange dyebath

Indigo vat

Old towels

Old newspapers

Iron

For this batik, I first used purple basil to dye a piece of silk fabric beige. After the fabric dried, I used lukewarm osage orange and indigo dyebaths to make a range of yellows and greens on the silk. Because batik designs are made by waxing fabrics, I chose colors that would penetrate the fibers without the need for high temperatures, which would melt the wax. The combination of these two dyebaths on the beige silk produced a wide range of colors. For sample, see page 127.

A Word About Materials

◆ Be sure to have baking soda at hand in order to extinguish a possible flash fire if the wax overheats.
◆ Use newspapers that are at least one month old; more recent papers are likely to transfer their inks to your fabric.

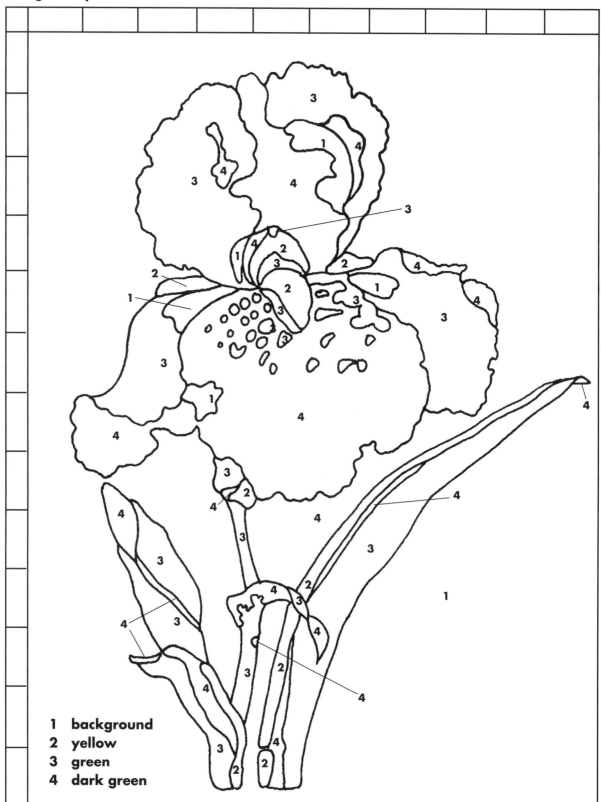

1 background
2 yellow
3 green
4 dark green

1. Dye the mordanted silk fabric in a purple basil dyebath, and allow it to dry.

2. Enlarge the pattern (see page 147 for tips on how to do this), and use heavy marker to darken pattern lines. Place the silk fabric over the pattern and trace lightly with pencil.

3. Stretch the fabric tightly over a frame to assure even wax penetration.

4. Following the pattern, wax area labelled "background." This area will not receive any additional dye. Check the underside of fabric to make sure the wax has thoroughly penetrated the fabric. Rewax portions on back of fabric where wax didn't penetrate. If the wax is opaque when brushed onto the silk, it is not hot enough, and it will thus not penetrate properly.

Wax melts at 90° F and ignites at 400° F. Be sure that the wax doesn't overheat. Turn down the heat if it begins to smoke.

---

5. Remove fabric from frame. Let the fabric sit in a pan of warm (not hot) water until it is well wetted.

6. Remove the fabric from the water, let it drip, and then put it into a strong, lukewarm osage orange dyebath. Make sure the dyebath is under 160°F, or the wax will disintegrate. If the wax starts to come off the fabric and float in water, the dyebath is too hot. Cool dyebath before reentering fabric.

7. Remove the fabric from the dyebath after 45 minutes, rinse in warm water, and lay fabric flat on an old towel to dry. If the color is not dark enough, repeat step 6. Blot off excess water with a towel.

8. When the fabric is dry, re-attach it to the frame. Wax areas marked "yellow" on diagram.

9. Remove fabric from frame. Wet fabric with warm water, and dip it into the indigo bath for approximately 30 seconds. If the fabric is too large to fit into your vat, dip one end, remove it, and then dip the opposite end.

10. Rinse the fabric and lay it flat to dry.

11. When dry, re-attach fabric to frame. Wax areas marked "green" on diagram.

12. Remove fabric from frame, and wet it with warm water. Dip it into the indigo vat again for approximately 1 minute.

13. Rinse fabric again, and lay it flat to dry.

14. When fabric is thoroughly dry, re-attach it to frame. Wax over areas labelled "dark green" on diagram.

15. Remove fabric from frame. Wet it with warm water, and dip once again into the indigo vat for approximately 30 seconds.

16. When the fabric is thoroughly dry, re-attach it to frame. Paint wax over the entire surface.

17. Remove the fabric from the frame. Hold it under cold water and scrunch it up to crack the wax coating. Make a final dip into the indigo vat to create the characteristic tiny crackle lines running through the batik. Lay out the fabric to dry thoroughly.

18. For the final step, be sure your work room has good ventilation. Place the fabric between several sheets of old newspaper, and iron it with a hot iron until the wax is dissolved and removed from the fabric.

19. Mount or frame the batik as desired.

Handmade Notepapers from Recycled Papers

— Materials —

Two pairs of wooden stretcher bars, 10" x 10" each (from an art-supply store)

Large staple gun

Rustproof wire screening

White scrap paper

Measuring cups

Old blender

Jars (quart and gallon size) and bucket

Apron

Natural dye liquors

Small strainer

Knife or spatula

Large sponge

Sheet of Plexiglas or cookie sheet with nonstick surface

Optional natural fibers; grasses, finely torn rags, pine needles, flower petals – fresh or dried, pressed flowers or leaves, shredded inner bark, etc.

Although this is a slightly unorthodox method for making handmade paper, it does serve as an easy-to-do introduction to the craft. Making your own paper is simple and a good way to experiment with the possibilities of natural dyes. The papers can be used for notepaper, gift enclosures, or paper-quilt greeting cards, or in collages. And, these papers not only look good, they smell good, too.

Because recycled fibers are used in these papers, they do not make archival quality papers. For the scrap paper base, 100 percent cotton paper is preferred, but any paper with at least 25 percent cotton content can be used. For the sample papers shown on page 127, I used logwood, cochineal, chamomile, brazilwood, purple basil, turmeric, and Mexican Mint marigold dyes.

You will need a smooth surface on which to dry the paper. A large plastic lighting diffuser or a sheet of Plexiglas is ideal. Flat cookie sheets are acceptable, although the paper may stick unless the pan has a nonstick surface, such as Teflon or Silverstone.

Making the paper mold

1. Join the four pieces of the wooden stretcher bars. Staple at the corners for stability.
2. As if you were stretching a canvas onto a frame, stretch the wire screen taut on top of the wooden frame. Staple around all edges, pulling as tight as possible.

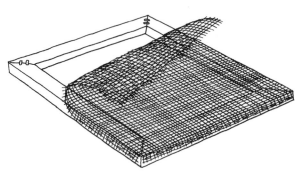

Stretching wire screening onto frame

Making the paper

3. Cut or tear white scrap paper into small pieces approximately 1" x 1". Cut enough pieces to fill a ½-gallon container, depending on how much paper you want to make.
4. Cover paper with warm water and soak overnight.
5. Put 1 cup of the soaked paper pieces into the blender, and fill almost to top with additional warm water. Turn the blender on for short bursts of speed until the pulp has been reduced to individual fibers. To evaluate whether the pulp is ready, put a small amount in a glass jar and hold it up to a light source. If you can see the individual fibers floating about in the water, the pulp is ready. If not, give it a few more turns in the blender.
   Note: Some pulps have a tendency to "foam up" in the blender, but it doesn't seem to have any effect on the resulting piece of paper. The foam can be skimmed off the top and discarded, or simply ignored.
6. Pour this mixture into a larger container and repeat step 5 several more times.
7. Strain the water from the pulp, and put the pulp back into the blender. Pour in dye liquor, and blend for several seconds or until well mixed. Let soak overnight in a glass jar.
8. Pour 1 cup of dyed pulp back into blender, add 4 cups of water, and mix for a few seconds.
9. With paper mold held over sink, pour contents of blender onto mold, making a rectangular shape while pouring. You can gently shape the pulp into place on the mold with the edge of a flat knife, if you wish.

Pouring dyed pulp onto mold

10. Let the pulp drain for a few minutes, and then press gently on the under side with a sponge to help squeeze out excess water.

Add Some Texture

Other items, such as glitter or mica flakes can be added to the paper pulp either before or after pouring. Some of the sample papers were decorated with leaves from the dyeplant used to color the pulp. Simply snip a few sprigs into the pulp before blending for the last time, right before pouring the pulp onto the mold.

Let the pulp drain for a few more minutes. (The water will drain away faster if the mold is slightly tilted.)

11. After paper piece has been sponged of all excess water, turn the mold upside down on a smooth surface. Sponge the back of the mold, pressing so that the paper adheres to the surface. The paper should release easily and fall off the mold at this point.

12. Gently remove the mold, first lifting one edge, and then the other. Gently sponge excess water from the paper and leave it until dry.

13. When the paper is completely dry, peel it from the surface. (It will tend to stick and tear if not yet dry.) One side will be very smooth and one side will be more textured. The thinner the paper, the faster it will dry.

For more information on papermaking, consult the following books:

The Art and Craft of Handmade Paper by Vance Studley (New York: Nostrand Reinhold, 1977)

The Art of Papermaking by Bernard Toale (Worcester, MA: Davis Publications, Inc., 1983)

Japanese Papermaking — Traditions, Tools, and Techniques by Timothy Barrett (New York: Weatherhill, 1983)

Making Your Own Paper by Marianne Saddington (Pownal, VT: Storey Communications, 1992)

Papermaking by Jules Heller (New York: Watson-Guptill, 1978)

Colors from Nature

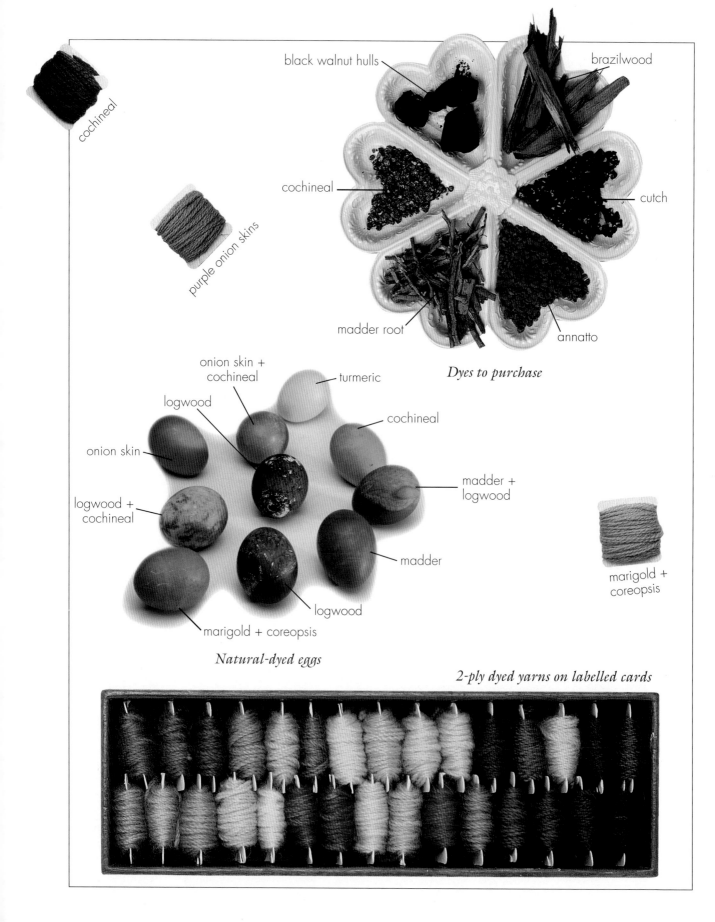

cochineal

purple onion skins

black walnut hulls

brazilwood

cochineal

cutch

madder root

annatto

Dyes to purchase

onion skin +
cochineal

turmeric

logwood

cochineal

onion skin

logwood +
cochineal

madder +
logwood

madder

logwood

marigold +
coreopsis

marigold +
coreopsis

Natural-dyed eggs

2-ply dyed yarns on labelled cards

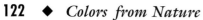

Around-the-World pillow

indigo

brazilwood

Cochineal-dyed skeins: (left to right) silk, wool, linen

Indigo

brazilwood + baking soda

Woven wool tapestry

Quilted wall hanging

logwood

osage orange
+ onion skins

Barberry

Natural-dyed embroidery floss

Black-eyed Susan

COREOPSIS

MADDE

MARIGOLD

Counted cross-stitch
notecards

Cornhusk wreath

koa

turmeric

Baby's First Garden crocheted blanket

osage orange extract

Lady's-bedstraw (with butter-and-eggs)

Lady's-bedstraw-dyed yarn

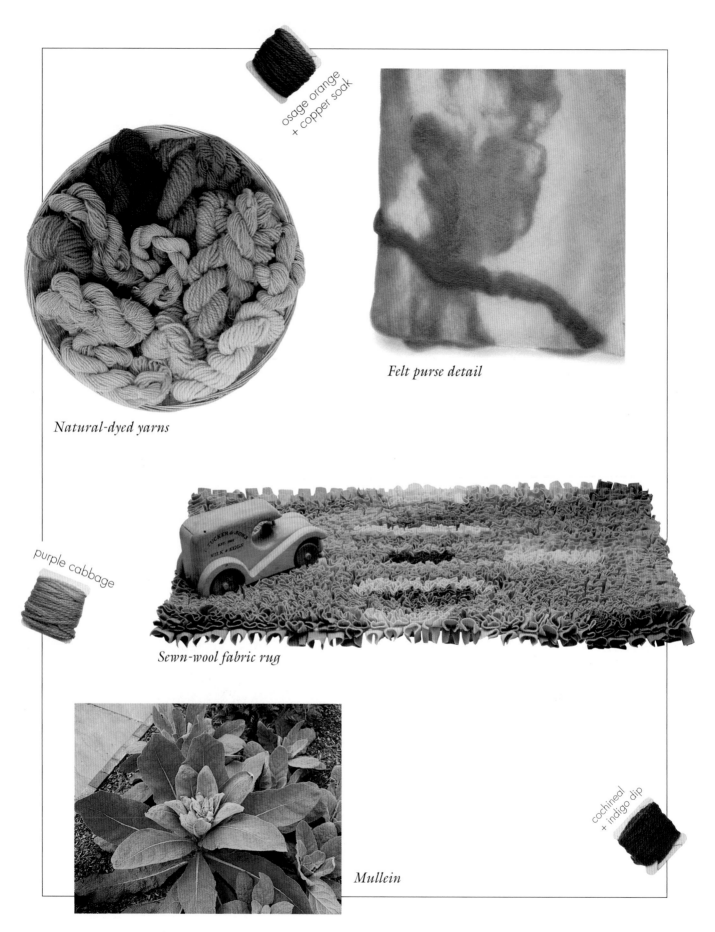

osage orange
+ copper soak

Felt purse detail

Natural-dyed yarns

purple cabbage

Sewn-wool fabric rug

cochineal
+ indigo dip

Mullein

Chamomile

*Confetti splint basket, with
madder- and indigo-dyed yarns*

chamomile

logwood

Brazilwood

cochineal

purple basil

Mexican mint marigold

chamomile

turmeric

spearmint

Mexican mint marigold

Batik on silk

Handmade note papers

purple onion
skins + short
indigo dip

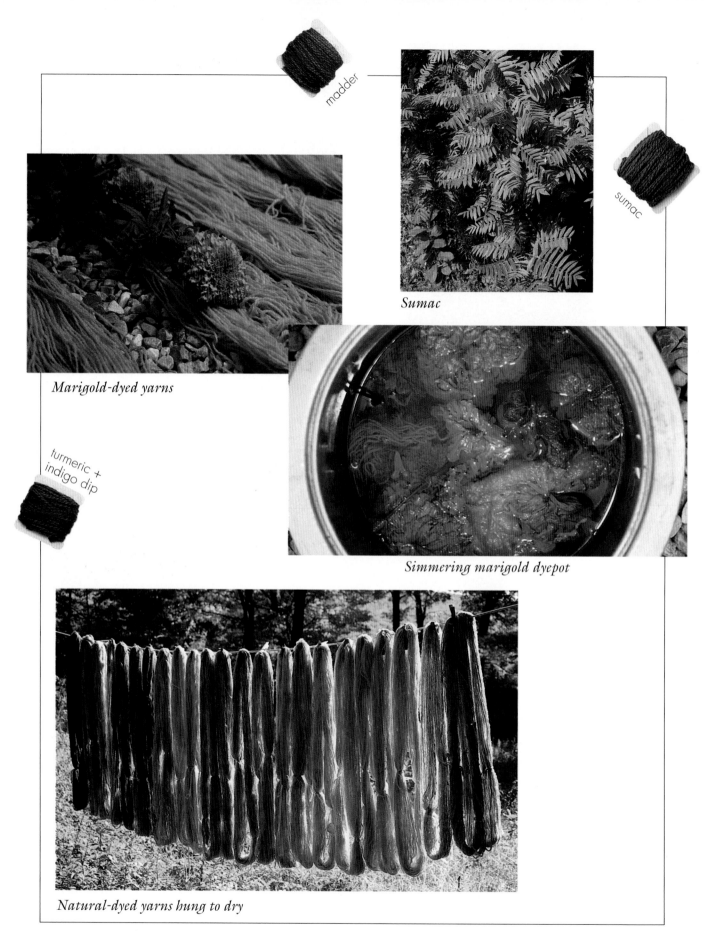

madder

sumac

Sumac

Marigold-dyed yarns

turmeric +
indigo dip

Simmering marigold dyepot

Natural-dyed yarns hung to dry

NOTE: The wrapped cards shown on these pages all carry yarns
mordanted with alum and cream of tartar, with the exception of the
indigo (p.123), the chamomile (p. 127), and the sumac (p. 128)
for which no assistants were used.

128 ◆ *Colors from Nature*

Felt Purse
with Silk Lining

Materials

Wool fleece carded in batts, white and various colors

Pieces of leftover dyed wool threads or yarns (optional)

Two pieces of cotton muslin or similar fabric, 29" x 42" and 26" x 28"

Large safety pins

Needle and thread

Rubber bands or strong string

Tub of hot water

Ivory dishwashing liquid or Fels Naphtha soap

Rubber gloves

Dyed silk fabric for lining, 10½" x 17"

Matching thread and needle

Velcro fastener or button and loop (optional)

Silk cord for handle (optional)

Ordinarily, when you scour fleece before dyeing, you must be very careful not to subject it to extremes in temperature or to handle it roughly. To make felt, you forget all of these rules on purpose! Shocking the wool fibers and thus making them shrink and bond together is what creates wool felt. Handmade wool felt can be used for a multitude of projects — from wall hangings and children's toys to warm booties and clothing. Felt is easy to cut and sew, and it doesn't ravel!

In the purse shown on page 126, I used yellow fleece dyed with turmeric; peach-colored fleece solar-dyed with brazilwood; blue dyed with indigo; and green dyed with turmeric and overdyed with indigo. I dyed the lining fabric with osage orange.

Creating the Felt

1. Follow the same procedure with both pieces of muslin. Lay the muslin on a flat surface. Put a thin layer of white fleece on

top of muslin with all fibers running in the same direction. For the larger piece of muslin, the first layer should be about 21" x 34" large. For the smaller piece of muslin, the fleece should be about 18" x 20". Leave at least a 4-inch border of muslin around all edges.

2. On top of first layer, lay a second layer of white fleece with the fibers running in the opposite direction (perpendicular) to the first layer. These two layers form the base of the felt piece. Make sure that there are no thin spots in the two layers. Fill in with more wool, if necessary.

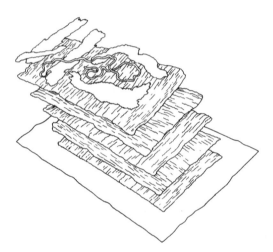

Layers of fleece and decorative yarns arranged on muslin

3. Build up additional layers of fleece, always placing the fibers in alternate directions. I used five layers of white fleece for the sample project. You can add more if you like, to make a thicker felt. The wool shrinks at least 30 to 50 percent when felted. If you have any doubt about how much you need, make more than enough. The finished piece can always be cut to size, if needed.

4. On top of the last layer, arrange handfuls of dyed fleece in a design of your choice.

Alternate Method of Decoration

Make the white felt backing first, and then re-felt the colored wools on top. This gives you a little better idea of what the design will look like when finished. Be aware, however, that the wools will not stick as well to the already-felted piece.

Some of them should be perpendicular to the last layer of white wool. Add scraps of wool yarns for additional surface interest.

5. Fold both side edges of muslin to overlap the fleece. Pin or stitch the corners together. (If you use safety pins, you can open up the bundle from time to time to check on the progress of the felting.)

6. Fold the top and bottom edges of muslin over the fleece, and pin or stitch along the sides, going through the layers of fleece. Mash the fleece down in order to fasten the two layers of muslin together securely.

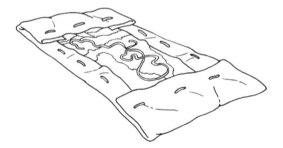

Folding muslin edges over layered fleece

7. Firmly roll up the fleece and muslin from bottom to top. Secure with rubber bands or tie with strong string.

8. Place fleece roll in sink or tub. Cover with hot or boiling water, and add several drops of Ivory dishwashing liquid or Fels Naphtha soap to the water. The soap helps speed up the felting process.

9. Knead the roll in the hot water until it is well soaked and soapy. Begin in the center and work out to the edges, squeezing the bundle as hard as possible. Use rubber gloves to protect your hands against the hot water.

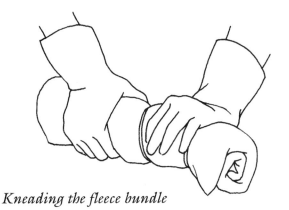

Kneading the fleece bundle

10. Plunge the roll into cold water. Continue to knead from the center to the ends. Squeeze out the excess water. Continue to knead the roll for approximately 10 minutes.

11. Repeat these hot and cold plunges. Knead for 10 more minutes. The more the fibers are "abused" the denser and firmer the piece of felt will be.

12. Unroll the bundle and examine the progress of the felting. Repeat the process until the piece has shrunk to ⅓ to ½ its original size and has matted together into a very dense piece.

13. Remove the felt from the muslin, and rinse under warm water to remove any remaining soap. The felt should be fairly strong at this point, but be careful not to stretch it.

14. Lay the felt out flat on a towel. Turn it periodically until it is thoroughly dry. Iron the felt using a pressing cloth, if desired.

Making the Purse

15. Cut one piece of felt to 10½" x 17" and the other to 9" x 9½".

16. Fold the larger piece of felt in half crosswise with right sides facing. Machine- or hand-stitch up both sides. Trim seams and turn piece right-side out.

17. Fold the silk lining piece crosswise and sew up sides. Trim seams.

18. Slip the silk lining inside the felt bag without turning.

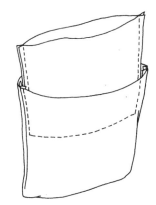

Slipping lining into turned purse

19. Turn down the top of the silk lining to the inside and pin. Use matching thread to slipstitch the lining to the felt, hiding the stitches inside the felt.

Hemming upper edge of lining against purse

20. To make the bag flap, stitch the smaller piece of felt to the top of the bag back.

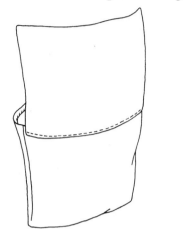

Stitching flap to purse

21. For closure, attach Velcro pieces or button and loop to the front of the bag, if desired. You may also add a wool or silk cord handle to the bag, if you wish.

Confetti Splint Basket

Materials

11 yards ⅜-inch flat reed, dyed tan (base)

2 yards ⅜-inch flat reed, dyed orange (weavers)

1 yard ⅜-inch flat reed, dyed blue (weaver)

3 yards ⅜-inch flat reed, dyed tan (weavers)

1 yard ⅜-inch flat reed, dyed blue (rim)

1 yard ⅜-inch flat reed, dyed orange (rim)

1 yard #5 round reed, dyed tan (rim filler)

2½ yards ³⁄₁₆-inch flat reed, dyed tan (lashing)

Corkboard

Stainless steel pushpins

Water mister or pan with warm water

Awl

Wooden spring-type clothespins

It's easy to dye wooden splints for your own homemade baskets, and the naturally dyed colors lend themselves well to these materials. The sample basket (page 127) was dyed tan (sumac), blue (indigo), and orange (madder) to make a combination of colors that reminds me of confetti.

When dyeing lengths of basketry materials for a specific project, it's a good idea to dye more than you estimate you'll need, in case of splitting or breakage. The extra can be used in other projects, for embellishing curls on the baskets, or for handles.

Basketry materials must remain damp and bendable while you are working with them. If they are too wet, however, they will split or shred. If you work the basket immediately after dyeing the materials and while they are still wet and flexible, you won't have to rewet the materials several times. If the pieces do begin to dry out, mist them lightly with a plant mister or dip the pieces momentarily into warm water before continuing.

Use an awl to help adjust spacing, pack weavers, and make a space for tucking in ends and lashings.

Preparing the Reed

1. Measure and cut the following pieces of reed:
   Eleven 19-inch pieces of tan (base)
   Nine 20-inch pieces of tan (base)
   Four 28-inch pieces of tan (weavers)
   Two 28-inch pieces of orange (weavers)
   One 28-inch piece of blue (weaver)
   One 28-inch piece of orange (rim)
   One 28-inch piece of blue (rim)
   Mark the centers of each of the base pieces.

Making the Basket Base

2. Pin the eleven 19-inch base pieces to the corkboard with the pushpins. Put the pin close to, but not through, the reed, as shown below. Leave a small gap in between each piece and make sure that the rough sides face up. (Basketry reed has both a smooth and a rough side.)

3. Working out from the center of these pieces, weave the nine 20-inch base pieces over and under. Leave a small gap between each one and place the rough side facing up. Center the 20-inch pieces over the 19-inch pieces. Use pushpins to hold the reed in place as it is woven in.

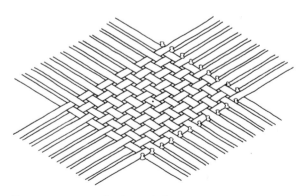

Base woven and pinned down

Weaving the Sides

4. Square up the corners and even the spacing. The base should measure 5¼" x 6½".
5. Gently fold up each spoke of the base, creasing the reed at the outer edge of the woven base to form the basket sides. This is called *upsetting the stakes*. If you wish, lay a straight edge alongside the base as a guide over which to bend the reed. Use clothespins to hold the corner spokes upright.

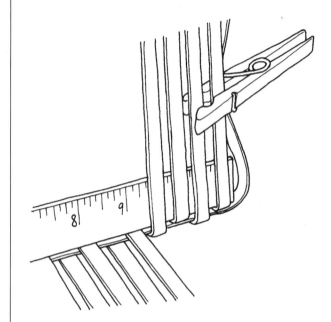

Upsetting the stakes

6. Weave a 28-inch tan weaver under and over (smooth side out) at the very bottom, along the creases of the base pieces. Be sure to keep in the weaving pattern established on the base. Go all the way around the base of the basket to the starting point. Overlap the reed ends several inches, and hide them behind upright side spokes. Trim excess. (See illustration next page, top.)

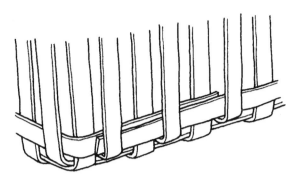

First row of weaving on side

7. Turn the basket one-quarter around, and repeat step 6 using weavers in the following order: tan, tan, orange, blue, orange, tan. Use an awl to pack each row down as tightly as possible to the previous row. Keep the tension equal from row to row to maintain straight sides, but allow the oval shape to develop. Even all spacing, make sure all spokes are absolutely vertical, and adjust shape, if necessary. After the basket dries, the reed will shrink in width, so spaces between rows will be larger than when wet. The sample project purposely was not packed very tightly in order to make a more open, airy weave.

Creating the Rim

8. Take all spokes that are over the last row, bend them to the inside, and tuck them into the third row of weaving. You may wish to cut the end of the spoke on an angle to make it slide into the weaving more easily. Trim the ends even with the bottom of the weaver. Cut off all of the remaining spokes even with the top of the basket. (See illustration top of next column.)

9. Place a blue weaver on the outside of the top weaver and an orange weaver on the inside. Begin and end these on opposite

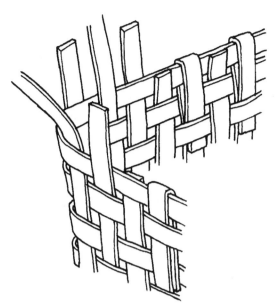

Trimming ends and weaving outside ends to inside

ends of the basket. Use clothespins to hold them in place. (The last tan weaver at the top of the basket is the "filling" in the "sandwich" formed by these two pieces. See illustration below.)

10. Place the round reed on top of these. Measure it to fit exactly and cut it on an angle to form a tapered join.

11. Use the ³⁄₁₆-inch flat reed to lash the rim pieces together, as shown.

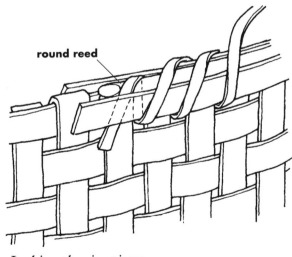

round reed

Lashing the rim pieces

Finishing Touches

12. On the inside of the basket, trim excess ends so that none is left sticking out. If the basket needs a bit of reshaping, do so while it is still damp. If the basket does not sit level, turn it upside down and weight it down with a heavy object, such as a large book, until it is dry.

13. Leave the basket to dry. After it is thoroughly dry, trim away any splinters or stray fibers with fingernail clippers or small scissors. Fill the basket with dyed balls of yarn, and enjoy!

Cornhusk Wreath

I used the following dyes in the sample project (shown on page 125): brazilwood for dark pinks and rose, purple cabbage for lavender, logwood for dark purple, onion skins for light yellows, and turmeric overdyed with indigo for greens. I combined many colors to show the potential of natural dyes on cornhusks, but a wreath with only one

▬ **Materials** ▬

A 12-inch round Styrofoam wreath base

A piece of heavy floral wire for hanger

Natural and dyed cornhusks

Scissors

U-shaped hairpins, cut to 1½ inches long with wire cutters

Floral pins

White household glue or hot glue

Rust-colored paper ribbon for bow (about 1 yard)

dyed color combined with natural-colored husks would also be lovely. You can also cut scallops or points at the ends of the petals. You'll find that the cornhusks are fun to work with and actually look like real flower petals when wet. Experiment with your own shapes and color combinations.

Dried cornhusks are brittle and tear easily, so they must be soaked in order to make them pliable enough to work with. Soak the cornhusks in warm water for at least 10 minutes before using them. While you are working, leave them in the water or spread them on a towel to keep them damp.

1. Use heavy floral wire to make hanger for wreath, as shown.

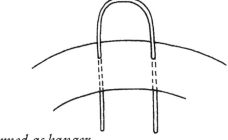

Wire formed as hanger

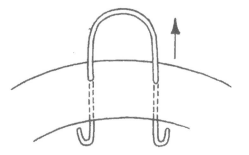

Hooked ends to attach

2. Cut the largest cornhusks in half from narrow to wide end (in direction of ribs). Snip off smaller ends.

3. Cover the wreath form with the cornhusk strips from step 2. Overlap the strips so that the form is well covered. Use the trimmed hairpins to fasten the ends in place on the back. The cornhusks shrink when dry, so make sure to overlap the ends at least ¾ inch.

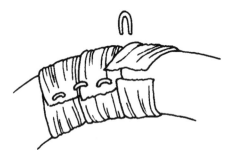

Covering the wreath form with cornhusk strips

4. Cut petal shapes from both natural and dyed husks using the pattern provided. (Up to six husks can be layered together and cut at the same time.) Cut the petals in the direction of the ribs, not crosswise. If pieces are cut crosswise, they will curl in the wrong direction and tear very easily. I used approximately 200 petals in the sample project — 100 natural and 100 dyed.

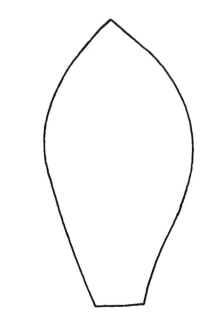

Petal pattern (actual size)

5. To attach the petals to the wreath, gather 5 or 6 together, alternating colors. Pinch ends together, and pin the bundle to the top surface of the wreath with floral pins.

Attaching the petal bundles to the wreath

Make sure pins are pushed firmly into wreath form. Since the wreath form is not very thick, angle the pins so that they do not come through on the sides, where they will show. Move around wreath, continuing to pin bundles on and overlapping bundles by about 1 inch. Point them all in the same direction. The tops of each petal bundle should cover the floral pin holding the previous bundle down.

6. When top of wreath is covered, repeat step 5 to cover the inner and outer edges of the wreath. If the petals become dry or start to curl, dip them into warm water for a few seconds to moisten them.

7. When the base is covered with petal bunches, gently fan some of the petals out, being careful not to pull them out.

8. Depending on your climate, it can take up to 48 hours for the husks to dry completely. When dry, check for bare spots on the wreath. The husks do shrink a bit when dry, so you may have to push some of the pins into the wreath form a little deeper to hold the bundles on. For greater security, put dabs of white household glue (or hot glue) on the ends of the cornhusks near the pins.

9. Make a bow with the paper ribbon, and attach it to the top of the wreath with a floral pin.

Cornhusk Angel

Cornhusk dolls are an American tradition. Although they are lovely in their natural state, I think they are even lovelier when dressed in cornhusks colored with natural dyes. I used the following dyes for the angel I made: brazilwood for dark pinks and rose, purple cabbage for lavender, turmeric for yellow, and logwood for purples.

Soak the cornhusks in warm water for at least 10 minutes before using them. To keep them damp, leave them in the water or wrap them in a towel while you are working.

Materials

Natural and dyed cornhusks

1-inch diameter Styrofoam ball (for head)

Floral wire

Heavy-duty thread

Small piece of polyester fiberfill, cotton, or fleece (for chest)

Piece of dyed wool roving or carded fleece (for hair)

White household glue or hot glue

Heavy glass bottle (for stand)

Fine-tipped permanent marker

1. Cut two strips of husk 2" x 6". Insert a 4-inch length of wire into the Styrofoam ball. Lay the ball between the two strips of husk. Wrap tightly with heavy-duty

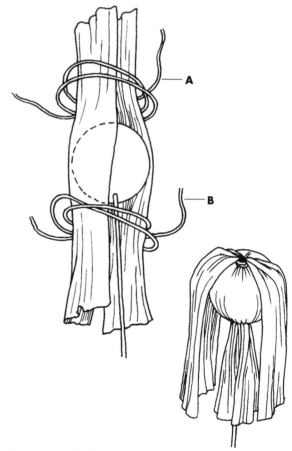

Forming the head

thread on both sides of the ball (at A and B in drawing). Pull the strips on the A side down over the uncovered parts of the ball to form the head.

2. Cut a piece of cornhusk 1" x 6". Roll the husk tightly around a 6-inch length of wire to form arms. Slip arms under the top layer of husk at the neck of the doll. Criss-cross thread over, under, and around arms and body to secure tightly.

3. Cut two 2" x 5" pieces of husk. Lay doll between husks with about 2 inches of husk extending above head. Wrap tightly at neck. Place a small piece of cotton at bustline. Pull strips down at front and back, and wrap tightly to form a waist.

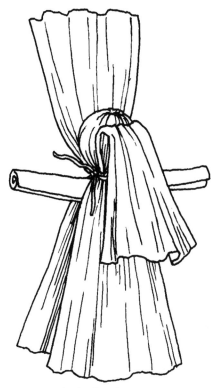

Pulling down the body pieces

4. Bend arms of doll upward.
5. Use a dark-colored cornhusk for an apron. Lay it on upside down, with bottom end over doll's head. Gather it around the waist and tie securely.

6. Make the skirt by layering colored husks over natural husks. Use about five or six of your widest pieces for the skirt and alternate colors as desired. Tie securely around waist. Pull husks down one layer at a time. The apron should lie neatly over the skirt.

Pulling down the apron and skirt pieces

7. To create angel wings, center a 5" x 6" piece of dyed husk over a larger, natural-colored piece of husk. Pinch together in middle, accordion style, and secure tightly with thread. (See wings in drawing on page 142.)

8. To cover gaps at shoulders and anchor wings in place, lay pieces of cornhusk over each shoulder, and lap them a little at

front and back for a shawl effect. Hold wings underneath this piece at the back. Tie shawl securely around waist. Wrap thin strips of cornhusk around waist to cover thread and form a sash.

9. Position the doll's arms and hands in front as desired. Trim cornhusks as necessary. Doll should be about 5 inches tall.

10. For hair, glue a small piece of dyed fleece to the top of the doll's head, styling as desired.

11. Place doll on a bottle until dry; after she dries, she should be able to stand on her own.

12. Use a fine-tipped black permanent marker to add features to the doll's face.

Tying on wings, shawl, and sash

Completed cornhusk angel

Naturally Dyed Easter Eggs

Although eggs are not exactly "natural fibers," children do love this project so I included it as a good one for introducing them to natural dyeing. It's an easy, one-step process that makes lovely colors that look just like real bird eggs! Many natural dyes work well on eggs. I've had good results with madder, onion skins, logwood, cochineal, marigolds, and turmeric. This is a great way to use up leftover dyebaths from other projects. Because of the possibility of allergic reactions from plant materials, I recommend using natural-dyed eggs for decorative purposes only, even if you use only nontoxic materials.

Although I usually use plain white vinegar to help set the colors on the eggs, I have also substituted apple cider vinegar. The apple cider vinegar shifts the normal purple logwood color to an unexpected, beautiful deep blue.

If store-bought (commercially produced), rather than farm-fresh, eggs are used, wash them first with dishwashing soap and a bit of vinegar. Eggs are sometimes coated with an oily substance before shipment to grocery stores, and this substance can cause the eggshells to resist the dyes, or the dyes may blotch or powder after they are dry. Washing the eggs in vinegar and soap sometimes helps to remove this film so that the eggs are more easily dyed.

Materials

Dye materials

Enamel or stainless steel pot

Eggs (at room temperature, to avoid cracking)

White vinegar (or apple cider vinegar)

Sprigs of plant material (optional)

Old pieces of hosiery or small pieces of muslin (optional)

1. Put a handful of dye materials into a pan. Add the eggs and several tablespoons of vinegar, and cover with water.
2. Heat the water to boiling, and simmer from 20 to 45 minutes, depending on the depth of color desired.
3. Remove the eggs from the water and cool undisturbed. Or, if you wish, leave the eggs in the dyebath to cool.

It is traditional to use the juice from the purple flowers of pasque flowers (Anemone pulsatilla) to make a green dye to color Pascal (Easter) eggs.

Plant Materials to Try with Eggs

Annatto seeds	Marigolds
Brazilwood	Onion skins
Coffee	Purple basil
Cosmos	Red cabbage
Logwood	Tea
Madder	Turmeric

Give your eggs a bright shine by rubbing them with cooking oil and then giving them a gentle buffing.

Decorated Eggs

- Press leaves against the eggs and wrap them securely in muslin or old knee-high hose before dyeing. The outlines of the leaves will remain white, and the rest of the egg will be colored with the dye.
- Overdye on eggs just as you do fibers. One of the sample eggs shown on page 122 was dyed in madder, then wrapped in spruce sprigs and put into a piece of stocking. The egg was then overdyed in logwood. The result is a two-color egg, embellished with the outline of the spruce leaves.
- Make batik eggs by writing or drawing on them with hot wax before dyeing. They must be dyed in a dyebath, such as madder, that does not need to be boiled to be effective, in order not to melt the wax before the design is imprinted on the egg.

Appendixes

Note on Copying and Enlarging Patterns

Some of the patterns in this book may be used actual size. If you wish to enlarge (or reduce) any of them, the easiest way to do so is to use the enlargement/reduction feature on a photocopier. If you don't have access to such a machine, mark a grid on the pattern. You will find guide marks along the top and down the left sides of some of the patterns for this purpose. Draw lines out from these marks to complete the grid, making sure that the vertical and horizontal lines are perpendicular to each other.

Calculate the size to which you want to enlarge (or reduce) the pattern, and make a grid on a blank sheet of paper whatever size is needed to produce the proper scale. Copy the pattern square by square.

APPENDIX II

Mail-Order Suppliers

Susan Bates, Inc.
212 Middlesex Avenue
Chester, CT 06412-0364

Anchor Embroidery Floss used in cross-stitch project

Beau Monde
Noel Clark
R.R. 1, Rte. 30, Box 687 (N. Rupert)
Pawlet, VT 05761

Dyes, mordants, fleeces, yarns, and spinning and weaving equipment

Blessing Historical Foundation
Ruth Pierce
Box 517
Blessing, TX 77419
512-588-6332

Madder seeds

The Corn Crib
R.R. 2, Box 164
Madison, MO 65263
314-682-2002

Natural cornhusks in 2-ounce, 4-ounce, or 1-pound packages (send a long SASE for further information.)

Creek Water Wool Works
Don McGill
P.O. Box 716
Salem, OR 97308

Dye extracts, mordants, yarns, and wools suitable for dyeing

Earth Guild
Bud Crawford
33 Haywood Street
Asheville, NC 28801

A "Mordanting Starter Set," as well as other dyes, books, and supplies

Frontier Cooperative Herbs
P.O. Box 299
Norway, IA 52318

Dried herbs and botanicals (including safflower and eucalyptus)

Harrisville Designs
Main Street
Harrisville, NH 03450

Manufacturers of the Harrisville Friendly Lap Loom used in tapestry project

Henry's Attic
Henry or Samira Galler
5 Mercury Avenue
Monroe, NY 10950
914-783-3930

Natural fiber yarns suitable for dyeing

Homegrown Colors
Sarah Plocher
580 S. Emerson
Denver, CO 80209

Dried dyes: cosmos, weld, pulverized madder roots, and so on

Lee S. McDonald, Inc.
Fine Hand Papermaking and Equipment
P.O. Box 264
Charlestown, MA 02129
617-242-2505

Papermaking supplies, fibers, molds, and so on

Meadows Wool Wash
Dalbo, MN 55017
612-389-5053

Manufacturers of Meadows French Lavender Wool Wash and Meadows Fibermaster Ultra Grease & Stain Formula

Richters
Box 26
Goodwood, Ontario
Canada L0C 1A0
416-640-6677

Many dye plants and seeds, including madder

Rio Grande Weaving Supply
Rachel Brown
216B Pueblo Norte
Taos, NM 87571
505-758-0433

General spinning and weaving supplies, and natural dyes and dye supplies, including mordants

Rumpelstiltskin
Linda Urquhart
1021 R. Street
Sacramento, CA 95814
916-442-9225

Natural dyes and general spinning and weaving supplies

Sammen Sheep Farm
Ron and Teresa Parker
Rt. 1, Box 153
Henning, MN 56551
218-583-2419

Spinning wools and wool batts

Soltec, Inc.
Redding, CT 06875

Manufacturers of Lano-Rinse and Lano-Wash

Taylor's Herb Gardens, Inc.
1535 Lone Oak Rd.
Vista, CA 92084
619-727-3485

Herb seeds and plants, many of which are dyeplants

Testfabrics
P.O. Box 420
Middlesex, NJ 08846
908-469-6446

"Ready-to-dye" fabrics — wools, cottons, silks, linens, and so on

Twinrocker Handmade Paper
P.O. Box 413
Brookston, IN 47923
317-563-3119

Papermaking supplies, fibers, molds, and so on

Well Sweep Herb Farm
317 Mt. Bethel Rd.
Port Murray, NJ 07865

Herb plants and seeds, many of which are dyeplants

Willmaur Crafts Corporation
735 Old York Rd.
Willow Grove, PA 19090
215-659-8702

Cut-out needlework greeting cards and envelopes

Wyrttun Ward
Gilbert A. Bliss
18 Beach Street
Middleboro, MA 02346

Herb plants and seeds, many of which are dyeplants

Yarn Tree Designs, Inc.
P.O. Box 724
Ames, IA 50010
515-232-3121

Cut-out needlework greeting cards and envelopes

APPENDIX III

Suggested Reading

Adrosko, Rita J. *Natural Dyes and Home Dyeing.* New York: Dover Publications, 1971.

Baker, Chris D., editor. *Herb and Spice Handbook.* Norway, IA: Frontier Herbs, 1987.

Bliss, Anne. "Dyeing in the Rockies." *Shuttle, Spindle & Dyepot,* Winter 1976.

_____. *A Handbook of Dyes from Natural Materials.* New York: Charles Scribner's Sons, 1981.

_____. *North American Dye Plants.* Boulder, CO: Juniper House, 1986.

_____. *Weeds: A Guide for Dyers and Herbalists.* Boulder, CO: Juniper House, 1978.

Brown, Rachel. *The Weaving, Spinning & Dyeing Book.* New York: Alfred A. Knopf, 1987.

Buchanan, Rita, editor. *Dyes from Nature.* New York: Brooklyn Botanic Garden, 1990.

_____. *A Weaver's Garden.* Loveland, CO: Interweave Press, 1987.

Casselman, Karen Leigh. *Craft of the Dyer: Colour from Plants and Lichens of the Northeast.* New York: Dover Publications, 1993.

Clausen, Ruth Rogers, and Nicolas H. Ekstrom. *Perennials for American Gardens.* New York: Random House, 1989.

Green, Judy. *Natural Dyes from Northwest Plants.* McMinnville, OR: Robin and Ross Handweavers, 1975.

Held, Shirley. *Weaving: A Handbook of the Fiber Arts.* New York: Holt, Rinehart and Winston, 1978.

Hurry, Jamieson B. *The Woad Plant and Its Dye.* Distributed by The Unicorn, Petaluma, CA, 1986.

Jacobs, Betty E. M. *Growing Herbs and Plants for Dyeing.* Distributed by The Unicorn, Petaluma, CA, 1982.

Jones, Pamela. *Just Weeds: History, Myths, and Uses.* New York: Prentice Hall Press, 1991.

Kierstead, Sallie Pease. *Natural Dyes.* Branden Press, 1972.

Liles, Jim N. *The Art and Craft of Natural Dyeing: Traditional Recipes for Modern Use.* Knoxville, TN: University of Tennessee Press, 1990.

McRae, Bobbi A. *Nature's Dyepot: A Resource Guide for Spinners, Weavers & Dyers.* Austin, TX: Fiberworks Publications, 1991.

Miller, Dorothy. *Indigo From Seed to Dye.* Aptos, CA: Indigo Press, 1984.

Robertson, Seonaid. *Dyes from Plants.* New York: Van Nostrand Reinhold, 1978.

Simmons, Adelma Grenier. *Herb Gardens of Delight.* New York: Hawthorn Books, Inc., 1974.

Tull, Delena. *A Practical Guide to Edible & Useful Plants.* Austin, TX: Gulf Publishing, 1987.

APPENDIX IV

Credits

See Appendix II for suppliers' addresses

"Baby's First Garden" Crochet Blanket and Pillow

Designed by Bobbi A. McRae and Barbara A. Neal

Sample project crocheted by Barbara A. Neal

Yarn courtesy of Don McGill at Creek Water Wool Works

Cotton Wall Quilt

Cotton fabrics courtesy of Testfabrics

Woven Wool Tapestry

Wool yarns courtesy of Rachel Brown, Rio Grande Weaving Supply and Henry Galler of Henry's Attic

"Friendly Lap Loom" courtesy of Harrisville Designs

Batik on Silk

Silk fabric courtesy of Testfabrics

Felt Purse with Silk Lining

Wool fleece courtesy of Teresa Parker, Sammen Sheep Farm

Silk courtesy of Testfabrics

Counted Cross-Stitch Dye Plant Notecards

Embroidery flosses courtesy of Susan Bates, Inc.

Notecards courtesy of Willmaur Crafts Corporation and Yarn Tree Designs, Inc.

Cornhusk Wreath

Cornhusks courtesy of The Corn Crib

Glossary

Adjective. A natural dye that needs mordants to permanently fix it to the fiber; also known as mordant dye

Alum. Aluminum potassium sulfate; aluminum ammonium sulphate

Bloom. To brighten a dyed color, usually by adding tin (stannous chloride) in the last few minutes of the dyebath or as an afterbath

Chrome. Bichromate of potash; potassium dichromate; potassium bichromate

Copper sulfate. Bluestone; blue vitriol

Cream of tartar. Tartaric acid

Crocking. Rubbing-off of a dye from the fiber; usually caused by improper rinsing of mordant

Cutch. Source of brown dye; from the heartwood of the *Acacia catechu*

Dyebath. The dye matter from the plant mixed with a certain amount of water

Dye liquor. The concentrated natural dye; the dye *ooze*

Fugitive. A dye that cannot be fixed permanently on the fiber; a dye that fades quickly

Glauber's salt. Hydrated sodium sulfate; used to "level" dyebaths

Iron. Also called copperas; green vitriol; ferrous sulfate

Mordant. Mineral salt that binds the dye to the wool and makes the color permanent

Natural dye. A dye obtained from a plant, animal, or mineral source

Overdye. To dye one color over another to create a third color

Sadden. To dull a color, usually done by using iron in the last few minutes of the dyebath or as an afterbath.

Scour. To wash and/or boil a fiber until natural oils, greases, and other substances are removed

Sodium benzoate. A preservative used in preserving dyebaths

Solution. A mixture of water and chemical or assistant

Substantive. A dye that requires no mordants; includes turmeric, black walnut hulls, oak bark and galls, and lichens

Tin. Also called stannous chloride

Top-dye. See Overdye

Index

(Illustrations are indicated by page numbers in *italics;* charts and tables by page numbers in **bold**).

A

Absinthe, **5–6**
Acacia catechu. See Cutch
Acacia koa. See Koa
Acetic acid. *See* Vinegar
Achillea millefolium. See Yarrow
Achiote. *See* Annatto
Additive. *See* Assistants
Adjective, 50, 152
Adrosko, Rita J.: *Natural Dyes and Home Dyeing,* 5
Afterbath, 57
Agrimonia eupatoria. See Agrimony
Agrimonia odorato. See Agrimony
Agrimony, **6,** *58, 72, 72*
Alder, **6, 58**
Alizarin, 75
Alkanet, **6,** *86, 86*
Alkanet tinctoria. See Alkanet
Allium cepa. See Onion skins
Alnus species. *See* Alder
Alum
    and cream of tartar, 42
    defined, 152
    described, 38, **40**
    formula, 45
    and sticky wool, 59
    and tannic acid, 47
Amaranth, **6**
Amaranthus species. *See* Amaranth
American nightshade. *See* Pokeweed
American saffron. *See* Safflower
American spinach. *See* Pokeweed
Ammonia, 42, 57
Anchusa tinctoria. See Alkanet
Angel, 140–142, *140, 141, 142*
Annatto, 7
    -dyed cornhusks, **53**
    overdyeing with, **56**
    purchased, 86–87, *122*
Anthemis nobilis. See Chamomile
Anthemis tinctoria. See Chamomile, dyer's
Anthocyanin, 60
Apple, **8**
Arctium minus. See Burdock
Arnatto. *See* Annatto
Around-the-World needlepoint pattern, 95–96, *96, 97, 123*
The Art and Craft of Natural Dyeing (Liles), 5, 47, 48
Artemisia absinthium. See Absinthe
Artemisia species. *See* Mugwort

Asclepias species. *See* Milkweed
Ash, 7, **58**
Asparagus, 7
Asparagus officinalis. See Asparagus
Aspen, **8, 58**
Asperula odorata. See Sweet woodruff
Asp of Jerusalem. *See* Woad
Assistants, 39, **40–41,** 42–43
Aster, **8, 58**
Aster species. *See* Aster

B

Baby's First Garden crochet pattern, 99–101, *100, 101*
Baking soda
    afterbath, 57
    as assistant, 42
Barberry, **8**
    cultivated, 70, *124*
    lightfastness of, **58**
    overdyeing with, **56**
    wild, 64
Barks
    dyeing with, 51–52
    harvesting, 63
    preserving, 78
Basic dyeplant chart, **5–27**
Basket making, *127,* 133–136, *134, 135*
Basketry fibers
    dyeing, 53–54, **54**
    mordanting, 48–49
    preparing, 36
Bastard saffron. *See* Safflower
Batik
    eggs, 144
    silk, 115–117, *116, 127*
Bayberry, **8, 58**
Bear's grape. *See* Pokeweed
Bedstraw, **8–9**
    cultivated, 72
    -dyed yarn, *125*
    lightfastness of, **58**
Beech, **9, 58**
Bennett, Jim, 53
Berberis species. *See* Barberry
Berries, 51, 63
Betony, **9**
Betula species. *See* Birch
Bicarbonate of soda. *See* Baking soda
Bindweed, **9,** 64, *64*

Birch, **9**
Bitter buttons. *See* Tansy
Bixa orellana. See Annatto
Blackberries, 63
Black-eyed Susan, *124*
    See also Coneflower
Black walnut, **10**
    -dyed basketry materials, 53
    lightfastness of, **58**
    overdyeing with, **56**, 64
    and solar dyeing, 55
    wild, 64
Blanket, 99–101, *100, 101, 125*
Bliss, Anne, vi, 43
    A Handbook of Dyes from Natural Materials, 5
Blocking, 96
Bloodroot, 53
Bloom, 39, 44, 152
Blue vitriol. *See* Copper
Bodark. *See* Osage orange
Bois d'arc. *See* Osage orange
Borax, 60
Boraxo. *See* Washing soda
Brassica oleracea. See Cabbage (purple)
Brassica species. *See* Cabbage (purple), Mustard
Brazilwood, **10**
    afterbath, 57
    -dyed notepaper, *127*
    -dyed yarn, *123*
    purchased, 87, *122*
    and solar dyeing, 55
Brighten. *See* Bloom
Broom, **10**
Buchanan, Rita, vi
    Dyes from Nature, 5, 44
    A Weaver's Garden, 48, 55, 75, 79, 81
Burdock, **10, 58**
Butter-and-eggs, *125*
    See also Toadflax
Butternut, 64

C

Cabbage (purple), **11, 58,** 83–84, *126*
Cactus fruit, 55
Caesalpinia echinata. See Brazilwood
Calliopsis. *See* Coreopsis
Campeachy wood dye. *See* Logwood
Candlewick plant. *See* Mullein
Cane, 48
Carrot, **11**
Carrot, wild. *See* Queen-Anne's-lace
Carthamus tinctorius. See Safflower
Casselman, Karen, vi
    Craft of the Dyer, 5, 47, 69, 84
Catnip, **11**
Cedar, **11**
Chamaemelum nobile. See Chamomile
Chamomile, **11–12**

cultivated, 73, *73, 127*
    -dyed notepaper, *127*
    -dyed yarn, *127*
Chamomile, dyer's, **12,** 73, *73*
Charts
    basic dyeplant, **5–27**
    dye results on basket splint, **54**
    dye results on cornhusks, **53**
    lightfastness, **58**
    mordanting, **40–41**
    overdyeing, **56**
    what went wrong?, **59**
Cheese rennet. *See* Bedstraw
Chemicals, 29, 31
    See also Mordants
Children and dyeing, 58, 143
Chlorophora tinctoria. See Fustic
Chrome, **40**
    ageing, 46
    defined, 152
    described, 38–39
    formula, 45
    and streaking, **59**
Chrysanthemum, **12**
Chrysanthemum parthenium. See Feverfew
Chrysanthemum species. *See* Chrysanthemum
Church steeples. *See* Agrimony
Coakum. *See* Pokeweed
Cochineal, **12–13**
    -dyed egg, *122*
    -dyed notepaper, *127*
    -dyed silk, *52*
    -dyed splint, **54**
    -dyed yarn, *122, 123, 126*
    lightfastness of, **58**
    overdyeing with, **56**
    purchased, 87, *122*
Cocklebur. *See* Agrimony
Coffea arabica. See Coffee
Coffee, **13, 53,** 84
Color
    combinations, **56,** 56–57
    and dyebath water, 60
    enhancement, **40–41**
    factors, 59–60, 63
    matching, 55, 98
    names, 51
    splotchiness, **59**
    See also Dye results, Dye sources
Colorfastness, **58,** 59
Coltsfoot, **13,** 65, *65*
Comfrey, **13**
Common wormwood. *See* Absinthe
Coneflower, **13–14, 58,** 73
Confetti splint basket, *127,* 133–136, *134, 135*
Continental stitch, 95, *95*
Continus coggygria. See Young fustic
Convolvulus arvensis. See Bindweed

Copper, 39, **40,** 45
Copperas. *See* Iron
Copper sulfate, 152
    See also Copper
Coreopsis, **14,** 51
    cross-stitch notecard, *104, 124*
    cultivated, 74, *74*
    -dyed cornhusks, **53**
    -dyed egg, *122*
    -dyed splint, **54**
    -dyed yarn, *122*
    lightfastness of, **58**
    and solar dyeing, 54
Coreopsis tinctoria. See Coreopsis
Cornhusk
    angel, 140–142, *140, 141, 142*
    dyeing, 53, **53**
    mordanting, 48–49
    preparing, 36
    wreath, *125,* 137–139, *137, 138*
Cosmos, **14,** 51, **58,** 74
Cosmos sulphureus. See Cosmos
Cotton
    dyeing, 52
    and Glauber's salt, 42
    mordanting, 39, 42, 47–48
    presoaking, 43
    washing, 35–36
Cotton wall hanging, 112–114, *112, 113, 124*
Cradlewort. *See* Bedstraw
Craft of the Dyer (Casselman), 5, 47, 69, 84
Cranberry, **14,** 84
Cream of tartar, 42, 152
Creeping jenny. *See* Bindweed
Crocheted blanket and pillow, 99–101, *100, 101, 125*
Crocking, **59,** 152
Cross-dyeing, 57
Cross-stitching, 102, 104–105
Cross-stitch notecards, 102–105, *103, 104, 105, 124*
Curcuma domestica. See Turmeric
Currant, **14**
Curry powder, **15**
Cutch, **15**
    defined, 152
    overdyeing with, **56**
    purchased, 87–88, *122*

D

Dactylopius coccus. See Cochineal
Dandelion, **15,** 51
    lightfastness of, **58**
    wild, 65, *65*
Daucus carota. See Queen-Anne's-lace
Daucus carota sativa. See Carrot
Digitalis purpurea. See Foxglove
Direct dyes, 50
Dock, **15,** 65, *65*
Drying rack, 29

Dull. *See* Sadden
Dyebath
    defined, 152
    exhaust, 60
    making, *50,* 50–52
    mordanting, 43–44
    plant ratio, 51
    preservation, 60
    water, 60
Dyed Easter eggs, *122,* 143–144, *144*
Dyed embroidery floss samples, *124*
Dyed yarn samples, 33, *121–128,*
Dye garden, 70, *71*
Dyeing steps, 28
Dye liquor, 152
Dye plant notecards, 102–105, *103, 104, 105, 124*
Dyeplants, **5–27,** 63, 64–69
    See also Dye sources
Dye pots, 29–30, 38
Dye results
    basket splint, **54**
    cornhusks, **53**
Dyer's alkanet. *See* Alkanet
Dyer's broom. *See* Broom
Dyer's chamomile. *See* Chamomile, dyer's
Dyer's coreopsis. *See* Coreopsis
Dyer's greenwood. *See* Broom
Dyer's marguerite. *See* Chamomile, dyer's
Dyer's mignonette. *See* Tansy
Dyer's rocket. *See* Tansy
Dyer's thistle. *See* Safflower
Dyes, natural. *See* Natural dye
Dyes, synthetic, 3
Dyes from Nature (Buchanan), 5, 44
Dye sources, **5–27,** 28, 51–52
    cultivated, 70–82
    food plant, 83–85
    purchased, 86–91, *122*
    wild, 64–69

E

Eggs
    decorated, 144, *144*
    dyed, *122,* 143–144
Elder, **15–16,** *65,* 65–66
Embroidery floss
    dyeing, 52
    mordanting, 47
    natural-dyed, *124*
Equipment, 28–30, *29*
Eupatorium purpureum. See Joe-Pye-weed
Exhaust baths, 60
Exotic hardwoods, 88

F

Fagus grandifolia. See Beech
False saffron. *See* Safflower
Fastness, **58,** 59

Felt making, 129–131, *130, 131*
Felt purse, *126,* 129–132, *130, 131, 132*
Fennel, **16**
Fermentation method, 55
Ferrous sulfate. *See* Iron
Feverfew, **16**
Field bindweed. *See* Bindweed
Flannel plant. *See* Mullein
Fleece
    dyeing, 35, 52
        felt making, 129–131, *130, 131*
        scouring, 35
Flowers, 51, 70, 78
Foeniculum vulgare. See Fennel
Food-plant dyes, 83
Foxglove, **16**
Fraxinus americana. See Ash
Fugitive, 152
Funnels, 30
Fustic, **16–17, 56,** 88

G

Galium verum. See Bedstraw
Garden plants, 70–82, *71*
Genista tinctoria. See Broom
Glauber's salt, 42, 152
Gloves, 29, 31
Golden marguerite. *See* Chamomile, dyer's
Goldenrod, **17,** 51
    cultivated, 74
    and solar dyeing, 55
    wild, 66, *66*
Granny square crochet pattern, 100, *100, 101*
Grape, **17,** 63, 66
Green vitriol. *See* Iron
Greenweed. *See* Broom
Grocery dyes, 83
Gum catechu. *See* Cutch

H

Haematoxylum brasiletto. See Brazilwood
Haematoxylum campechianum. See Logwood
A Handbook of Dyes from Natural Materials (Bliss), 5
Handmade notepapers, 118–120, *119, 127*
Hardwood dyes, 88
Harvesting dyeplants, 63–69
Hedge apple. *See* Osage orange
Held, Shirley: *Weaving,* 3, 46
Helianthus annuus. See Sunflower
Helianthus maximiliani. See Sunflower
Henna, **17,** 88
Herb-of-St.-John's. *See* St.-John's-wort
Herbs, 51
Holly grape, **17**
Hopi red dye. *See* Amaranth
Hops, **18,** 88
Horse apple. *See* Osage orange
Hose, 30

Humulus lupulus. See Hops
Hydrosulfite reduction, 89–90
Hypericum perforatum. See St.-John's-wort
Hypernic, 87

I

Indigo, **18**
    cultivated, 74–75, *123*
    dip, *126, 127, 128*
    -dyed cornhusks, **53,** 54
    -dyed silk, 52
    -dyed splint, **54**
    -dyed yarn, *123*
    overdyeing, **56,** 57, 90, *128*
    preserving, 78
    purchased, 89–90
    reduction, 89–90
Indigofera species. *See* Indigo
Indigo from Seed to Dye (Miller), 75
Indigotin, 81
Indigo white, 89
Inkberry. *See* Pokeweed
Insect dye. *See* Cochineal
Iron, **40**
    defined, 152
    described, 39
    formula, 45
    and silk, 48
Ironweed, **18**
Isatis tinctoria. See Woad

J

Japanese indigo, 75
Jars, 30
Joe-Pye-weed, **18**
Juglans cinerea. See Butternut
Juglans nigra. See Black walnut
Juniperus virginiana. See Cedar
Jute, 36

K

Kierstead, Sallie Pease: *Natural Dyes,* 48
Koa, **18,** *125*

L

Labels, 33
Lactuca species. *See* Lettuce
Lady's bedstraw, *125*
    See also Bedstraw
Lawsonia inermis. See Henna
Leaves
    as dye source, 51
    as egg decorations, 144, *144*
    preserving, 78
Lemon juice afterbath, 57
Lettuce, 84
Lightfastness, **58,** 59, 83
Liles, Jim N., vi

The Art and Craft of Natural Dyeing, 5, 47, 48
Linaria vulgaris. See Toadflax
Linen, 47–48
    cochineal-dyed, *123*
    See also Cotton
Litmus paper, 30, 60
Logwood, **18–19**
    afterbath, 57
    -dyed cornhusks, **53**
    -dyed egg, *122*
    -dyed notepaper, *127*
    -dyed silk, 52
    -dyed yarn, *124*
    purchased, 90
    and solar dyeing, 55
Lupulin, 88
Luteolin, 80
Lycopersicon lycopersicum. See Tomato

M

Maclura pomifera. See Osage orange
Madder, **19,** 52
    cross-stitch notecard, *105, 124*
    cultivated, *75,* 75–76
    -dyed cornhusks, **53**
    -dyed egg, *122*
    -dyed silk, 52
    -dyed splint, **54**
    -dyed yarn, *127, 127*
    overdyeing with, **56**
    purchased, 90–91, *122*
    and solar dyeing, 55
Mahonia species. *See* Holly grape
Mail-order suppliers, 148–149
Malus species. *See* Apple
Marigold, **19,** 51
    cross-stitch notecard, *103, 124*
    cultivated, 76–77
    -dyed cornhusks, **53**
    -dyed egg, *122*
    -dyed notepaper, *127*
    -dyed silk, 52
    -dyed splint, **54**
    -dyed yarn, *122, 128*
    dyepot, *128*
    and solar dyeing, 54, 55
Marjoram, **19**
Matching colors, 42, 55, 98
Measuring cups, 30
Mentha species. *See* Mint
Microwave
    drying, 78
    dyeing, 57–58
Milfoil. *See* Yarrow
Milkweed, **20,** 66
Miller, Dorothy, vi
    Indigo from Seed to Dye, 75
Mint, **20,** 51, 77, *77*

Mordanting
    dyebath, 43–44
    post-, 44
    solar, 54
    pre-, 43
        of basketry fibers, 48–49
        of cotton, 47
        of silk, 48
        of wool, 45–47
    top-, 55
Mordants, 38–39, **40–41**
    ageing, 46
    Colonial, 38
    dangers of, 30
    defined, 37, 152
    disposal of, 44
    Indian, 38
    storing, 31
    testing, 39
    uses for, **5–27, 40–41**
    wood ashes as, 38
    See also Alum, Chrome, Copper, Iron, Tin
Morus species. *See* Mulberry
Morus tinctoria. See Fustic
Mugwort, **20**
Mulberry, **20**
Mullein, **20–21**
    cultivated, 77, *126*
    overdyeing, **56**
    wild, 66
Mustard, **21,** *66,* 66–67
Myrica pensylvanica. See Bayberry

N

Natural dye
    classifications, 50
    defined, 152
    history, 3, 5
    sources, 5, **5–27,** 51–52
Natural-dyed embroidery floss, *124*
Natural-dyed yarns, *121, 126, 128*
Natural Dyes (Kierstead), 49
Natural Dyes and Home Dyeing (Adrosko), 5
Natural fibers, 33
    mordanting of, 43–44
Naturally dyed Easter eggs, *122,* 143–144, *144*
Needlepoint pillow, 95–98, *95, 96, 97, 123*
Nepeta cataria. See Catnip
Nettle, **21,** 67, *67*
New Herbal (Turner), 3
Nits-and-lice. *See* St.-John's-wort
Notecards, 102–105, *1–3, 104, 105 124*
Notepapers, 118–120, *119, 127*
Nuts
    harvesting, 63
    preserving, 78
    See also Black walnut

O

Oak, **21**, 67
Old fustic. *See* Fustic
Onion skins
   -dyed cornhusks, **53**
   -dyed egg, *122*
   -dyed yarn, *122, 124*
   as dye source, **21–22**, 51, 84–85
   overdyeing with, **56**
Origanum majorana. See Marjoram
Osage orange, **22**
   -dyed basketry materials, 53
   -dyed cornhusks, **53**
   -dyed splint, **54**
   -dyed yarn, *124, 125, 126*
   purchased, 91
Our Lady's bedstraw. *See* Bedstraw
Overdye, 55–57, **56**
   defined, 152
   with iron, 39
Overdyed eggs, 144
Overdyed yarn samples, *126, 127, 128*

P

Paper making, 118–120, *119*
Paste-resist technique, 113
Pattern copying, 147
Pear, **22**
pH balance, 60
Phytolacca americana. See Pokeweed
Pierce, Ruth, vi, 76
Pigeonberry. *See* Pokeweed
Pigweed. *See* Amaranth
Pillow making, 96, 98, *98*, 101, *123*
Plant material ratio, 51
The Plictho (Rosetti), 3
Plum, **23**
Pocanbush. *See* Pokeweed
Pokan. *See* Pokeweed
Pokeberry
   -dyed silk, 52
   overdyeing with, **56**
   See also Pokeweed
Poke salad. *See* Pokeweed
Pokeweed, **23**
   cultivated, 77–78
   wild, 67, *67*
   See also Pokeberry
Polygonum tinctorium. See Japanese indigo
Populus species. *See* Aspen
Postmordanting, 44, 54
Potassium aluminum sulfate. *See* Alum
Potassium dichromate. *See* Chrome
Pot covers, 31
Pots, 29–30, 38
A Practical Guide to Edible and Useful Plants (Tull), 5
Premordanting, 43
   of basket fibers, 48–49

   of cotton, 47
   of silk, 48
   of wool, 45–47
Preserving dyebaths, 60
Preserving dye materials, 78
Presoaking, 43
Projects
   angel, 140–142, *140, 141, 142*
   batik, 115–117, *116, 127*
   basket, *127*, 133–136, *134, 135*
   blanket, 99–101, *96, 97, 98, 125*
   Easter eggs, *122*, 143–144, *144*
   notecards, 102–105, *1–3, 104, 105, 124*
   notepapers, 118–120, *117, 127*
   pillow
      crocheted, 99–101, *96, 97, 98*
      needlepoint, 95–98, *100, 123*
   purse, *126*, 129–132, *130, 131, 132*
   rug, 109–111, *110, 111, 126*
   tapestry, 106–108, *107, 108, 123*
   wall hanging, 112–114, *112, 113, 124*
   wreath, *125*, 137–139, *137, 138*
Prunus domestica. See Plum
Purple basil
   -dyed cornhusks, **53**
   -dyed notepaper, *127*
Purple cabbage. *See* Cabbage (purple)
Purse making, 131–132, *131, 132*
Putrefaction dyeing, 55
Pyrus communis. See Pear

Q

Queen-Anne's-lace, **23**
Quercus species. *See* Oak
Quilted cotton wall hanging, 112–114, *112, 113, 124*

R

Raffia
   dyeing, 53
   mordanting, 48–49
   preparing, 36
Recordkeeping, 30–31, *32*
Recycled paper notepapers, 118–120, *117, 127*
Reduction, 89–90
Redweed. *See* Pokeweed
Redwood. *See* Brazilwood
Reed
   dyeing, 53
   preparing, 36
Reed basket, *127*, 133–136, *134, 135*
Reppert, Susanna, 53
Reseda luteola. See Weld
Rheum rhabarbarum. See Rhubarb
Rhubarb, **23**
Rhus glabra. See Sumac
Ribes species. *See* Currant
Roots
   as dye source, 51–52

harvesting, 63
    preserving, 78
Rosemary, **23**
Rosetti, Gionventura: *The Plictho,* 3
Rosmarinus officinalis. See Rosemary
Roucou. *See* Annatto
Rubia tinctorum. See Madder
Rudbeckia hirta. See Coneflower
Rudbeckia species. *See* Coneflower
Rug, sewn-wool, 109–111, *110, 111 126*
Rumex acetosa. See Sorrel
Rumex species. *See* Dock

S

Sadden, 152
    with copper, 39
    with iron, 39, 43, 44
Safety
    and batiking, 115, 117
    and children, 58
    and mordant disposal, 44
    precautions, 30, *31,* 39, **41**
Safflower, **24**
    cultivated, *78,* 78–79
    and solar dyeing, 55
Sage, **24,** 51, 79, *79*
St.-John's-wort, **24**
    cultivated, 79
    wild, 68, *68*
Sal soda. *See* Washing soda
Salt, as assistant, 42
Salvia officinalis. See Sage
Sambucus canadensis. See Elder
Sassafras, 53, **54**
Saxon green, 55
Scale, 30
Scour, 152
Scouring
    cotton, 35–36
    wool, 34–35
Sericin, 36
Sewn-wool fabric rug, 109–111, *110, 111, 126*
Silk
    cochineal-dyed, *123*
    degumming, 36
    dyeing, 52
    mordanting, 39, 48
Silk batik, 115–117, *116, 127*
Silk purse lining, 131
Sisal, 36, 53
Skein
    making, 33–34, *34*
    tying, 52
Soaps, 36
Sodium benzoate, 42, 60, 152
Sodium carbonate. *See* Washing soda
Sodium hydrosulfite, 89, 90
Sodium sulfate. *See* Glauber's salt

Solar dyeing, 54–55
Solidago canadensis. See Goldenrod
Solidago species. *See* Goldenrod
Solution, 152
Sorrel, **24**
Sowberry. *See* Barberry
Spearmint-dyed notepaper, *127*
Speckled John. *See* St.-John's-wort
Spices, **15**
    See also Curry powder
Spinach, 84
Spinacia species. *See* Spinach
Splint
    dyeing, 53, **54**
    mordanting, 48–49
    preparing, 36
    presoaking, 43
Splint basket, *127,* 133–136, *134, 135*
Spoons, 29
Stachys officinalis. See Betony
Stannous chloride. *See* Tin
Steeping, 55
Sticklewort. *See* Agrimony
Stinging nettle. *See* Nettle
Stirring rods, 29
Strainers, 30
Substantive, 152
    See also Direct dyes
Sumac, **24–25**
    -dyed splint, **54**
    -dyed yarn, *128*
    purchased, 90
    wild, 68, *128*
Summer broom. *See* Broom
Sunflower, **25,** 79–80, *80*
Suppliers, 148–149
Supplies, 28–30
Sweet marjoram. *See* Marjoram
Sweet woodruff, **25**
Symphytum officinale. See Comfrey

T

Tagetes species. *See* Marigold
Tanacetum vulgare. See Tansy
Tannic acid. *See* Tannin
Tannin, 39, **40,** 42, 45, 47
Tansy, **25,** 80, *80*
Tapestry, 106–108, *107, 108, 123*
Taraxacum officinale. See Dandelion
Tartaric acid. *See* Cream of tartar
Tea, **25–26,** 85
Thea sinensis. See Tea
Thermometer, 30
Thousand seal. *See* Yarrow
Thyme, **26**
Thymus vulgaris. See Thyme
Tickseed. *See* Coreopsis
Timer, 29

Tin, **40**
    and cream of tartar, 42
    defined, 152
    described, 39
    formula, 45
    and splotchiness, **59**
Toadflax, **26**
Tomato, **26**, *68*, 68–69
Topdye. *See* Overdye
Topmordant, 55
Tull, Delena: *A Practical Guide to Edible and Useful
    Plants*, 5
Turmeric, **26–27**, 85
    -dyed cornhusks, **53**
    -dyed egg, *122*
    -dyed notepaper, *127*
    -dyed silk, 52
    -dyed splint, **54**
    -dyed yarn, *125, 127*
    overdyeing with, **56**, 57
    and solar dyeing, 55
Turner, William: *New Herbal*, 3
Tussilago farfara. *See* Coltsfoot

U

Uncaria gambier. *See* Cutch
Urtica dioica. *See* Nettle
Urucu. *See* Annatto

V

Vaccinium macrocarpon. *See* Cranberry
Vat dyes, 50
Velvet plant. *See* Mullein
Verbascum blattarai. *See* Mullein
Verbascum thapsus. *See* Mullein
Vernonia species. *See* Ironweed
Vinegar
    afterbath, 57
    as assistant, 42
    as pH balancer, 60
Virginia poke. *See* Pokeweed
Vitis species. *See* Grape

W

Wall hanging, 112–114, *112, 113, 124*
Walnut hulls. *See* Black walnut
Washfastness, 59

Washing soda, 42
    and indigo reduction, 89–90
Water for dyeing, 60
A Weaver's Garden (Buchanan), 48, 55, 75, 79, 81
Weaving (Held), 3, 46
Weaving terminology, 106
Weiss, Martha, 60
Weld, **27**
    cultivated, *80*, 80–81
    -dyed silk, 52
    overdyeing with, 57
Wild carrot. *See* Queen-Anne's-lace
Wild grape. *See* Grape
Wild mustard. *See* Mustard
Wild snapdragon. *See* Toadflax
Woad, **27**, 70, 81, *81*
Woadwaxen. *See* Broom
Wood chips, 88
Wooden splint. *See* Splint
Wool
    brittle, **59**
    cochineal-dyed, *123*
    color matched, 42
    dyeing, 42, 52
    handling, 45
    mordant damaged, 39, 42, 44
    naturally colored, 55
    premordanting, 43, 45–47
    skeining, 33–34, *34*
    sticky, **59**
    washing, 34–35
Wool fabric mordanting, 47
Wool rug, 109–111, *110, 111, 126*
Wool tapestry, 106–108, *107, 108 123*
Wormwood. *See* Absinthe
Woven wool tapestry, 106–108, *107, 108 123*
Wreath, *125,* 137–139, *137, 138*

Y

Yarrow, **27**, 81, *81*
Yellow bedstraw. *See* Bedstraw
Yellow toadflax. *See* Toadflax
Young fustic, 88

Z

Zinnia, 51, 82
Zinnia species. *See* Zinnia